THE PROMISED LAND

COMPANION TO THE VEIL

ROSEMARY ARGENTE

© Rosemary Argente 2017

All rights reserved. No part of this book may be reproduced or transmitted in any form or by any means, electronic or mechanical, including photocopying, recording or by any information storage and retrieval system, without permission in writing from Simanyi Books or the author.

First edition 2017

Editor: Ann-Marie Budyn

Publishers: Asaina Books
Website: asainabooks.co.uk
Email: rosa@asainabooks.co.uk

Books by the same author:

Blantyre and Yawo Women
The Veil
The Promised Land - Companion to The Veil
Broken Temple
Praying Mantis
Difference
Share the Ride
Home From Home
Essays and Poetry
The Place Beyond
Caesar and Mapanga Homestead

Novels:
All Mine to Have
Farewell Sophomore
The Stream of Memory
A British Throne Scandal

Science Fiction:
Farewell to the Aeroplane

Booklets:
Journey of Discovery
Enduring Fountain - Health and Well-being
Katherine of the Wheel
Cooking With Asaina

Acknowledgements

My sincere thanks are due to my editor, Ann-Marie Budyn and to persons too numerous to mention, transcending faiths and cultures, for giving me much of their time in our discussions to share their personal views on matters of faith and religion. My thanks are also due to Ian Upton, David Duddle, Brian Sherman and Mark Sherman for their invaluable help on my struggles with technology and generally.

Rosemary Argente

Dumfries, 2017

CONTENTS

PROLOGUE 1
CHAPTER 1 Zechariah at the Golden Incense Altar 2
CHAPTER 2 Abrahamic Covenant 6
CHAPTER 3 Egypt's new Pharaoh 12
CHAPTER 4 Exodus 17
CHAPTER 5 The Sinai Desert 23
CHAPTER 6 The Era of Numbers passes 34
CHAPTER 7 The Biblical Number 42
CHAPTER 8 Solomon Inherits a powerful kingdom 47
CHAPTER 9 After Solomon's death 53
CHAPTER 10 Yochanan is born to Elikana & Elesheba 59
EPILOGUE 67

Prologue

IT WAS A TURNING POINT in my spiritual journey when my beautiful friend Lili died. We were both eight years old. Since then I have searched for an answer to the burning question that has much occupied my mind:

"Can a skilled artist make a beautiful ornament only to smash it in the end?"

The Bible holds fascinating stories but perhaps the most fascinating is the story of the *Tabernacle* of the Israelites which is symbolised to man's temporal journey of life through earth.

The tabernacle is set in a human drama where the specially chosen are cast as players in supporting roles to the lead player, the chosen one of the *New Covenant*. The *tabernacle* is not manifest in the beginning but in Genesis God said:

"Let us make man..." the statement is in the `plural', to whom was the Almighty speaking?

Abraham's concept of the *one true God* was followed by Moshe, chosen when he led the Israelite to the promised land during the Exodus on Mount Sinai. It was an earthly mobile temple, a visible object and a house for prayer. The purpose was to enable us to find the way back to the Almighty to regain Paradise lost. Over every stage through the eras of the tabernacle, some *specially chosen* emerge to perform a specific service in the spiritual language on earth capable of understanding in their heart.

The objects of the world are visible enabling us to understand the Almighty wonder of wisdom and spiritual direction. Intuitions and hunches are a sudden impulse of the spirit speaking the same language in the universal current of existence.

Everything in the universe evolved, the earth is alive and has a soul crammed with heaven; filled with mystical language as a clue to the way forward; and everything in it is continually transformed through a lineal *binding thread*.

CHAPTER 1

ZECHARIAH AT THE GOLDEN INCENSE ALTAR

ZECHARIAH IS CHOSEN BY LOT on that morning to offer incense at the Golden Altar of the *Holy Place* in the Temple. Upon another table is the magnificent lamp stand with its multiple torches (*menorah*), oil for the lamp, dishes, covers, spoons and bowls. On the golden tray displayed are two frankincense cups and the golden tray on which are *twelve* loaves of shewbread (twelve loaves placed every Sabbath in the Jewish Temple and eaten by the priests at the end of the week). The golden incense altar is the same one of acacia wood that was used by the Hebrew during the *Exodus*. It is now the thirteenth year in the reign of Herod the Great over Israel (37–4 BCE).

Though Zechariah may never serve at the *Holy of the Holies,* offering incense at prayer time in the *Holy Place* is a once in a lifetime privilege. He is dedicated to the Temple and both he and his wife Elisheba are descendants of Aaron. As Zechariah is praying the archangel Gabriel appears on the right side of the altar and tells him that his prayers for a child are answered and Elisheba is to have a child whom they shall call Yochanan.

Elesheba has passed the age of child bearing but still hopes for a son to follow in the footsteps of his father and carry on the ministry. She is scorned for being childless, not unlike Sarah, wife of Abraham, Rebekah of Isaac, Rachel of Jacob, and Hannah of Elikanah long before Elisheba's time.

Elisheba is blessed with the *Maternal Covenant*. During the sixth month of her pregnancy she is visited by her cousin Miriam. As Elisheba hears Miriam's greeting, the baby in her womb leaps. Miriam has called to tell her older cousin that she too is blessed with the *Maternal Covenant.* Six months after the birth of Yochanan, Miriam gives birth to a baby in a humble cattle shed at Bethlehem. Miriam and her husband Yosef place him in a feeding trough and name him Yeshua, meaning *God is salvation.*

****

THE TABERNACLE BEGINS with the call of Abram as head of the people when YAHWEH (God) made the `Abrahamic Covenant' with him in the administration of `Dispensation of Promise' as the basis for the development of future covenants on a Messiah-Redeemer yet to come given to the entire race in Adam.. This was God's work and purpose in an *orderly divinely ordained management* ODOM) of Israel and the Israelite in their religious system in given periods of time as custodians for all mankind. Future specific blood covenants were to be made between God and certain chosen persons when mankind is tested and warned of the consequences of disobedience. Salvation is by the grace of YAHWEH alone. A poetic person, Abram is founder of the one true *faith* to endure through the ages in spiritual direction. He was favoured to be father of many nations of the world as his descendants would spread to the west, east, north and south.

The *Edenic Covenant* was the first age of ODOM in the era of *Genesis* and `innocence' in a perfect environment. Adam and Eve broke the tenets: the *tree of life,* and *the tree of knowledge of good and evil.* They received the Judgment of Expulsion from the Garden of Eden. When God cursed Adam, Eve and descendants, the human body and everything else including the Earth itself became subject to death and decay. God remained forgiving and gave Adam and Eve a second chance.

The *Adamic Covenant,* the second age of ODOM in the era of `conscience' and the understanding of `good' and evil'. They were given the grace to honour the Creator by observing moral law written in their heart and conscience. Cherubim were placed at the east of the Garden of Eden, and a flaming sword which turns every way, guarding the way to the Tree of Life.

The *Noahic Covenant* was the third age of ODOM and 'human government' in the era of *Genesis* and man's responsibility to govern man for God, Jew and Gentile alike. Only the Gentiles govern for the purpose of establishing order, punish evil and promote justice. Despite the introduction of the *Adamic covenant,* in Noah's day, selfishness, corruption and violence abounded. Only Noah faithfully abided by the acts that pleased God.

Then God called upon Noah to build an Ark and God was to lay a flood to destroy a wicked world. Noah had never seen rain, for in that time a mist went up from the earth and irrigated the whole face of the ground for the growth of plants; and further, he could not visualise how the ark would float as he lived hundreds of miles away from the nearest sea. How he was to round up all the animals presented a further problem for Noah but he soldiered on placing complete trust in God.

He built an ark of gopher wood to float and save life and its size was 300 cubits length x 50 cubits width x 30 cubits height. It was covered with pitch inside and outside. Noah, his family, along with all species of selected male and female animals took refuge in the ark and he took provisions for their sustenance. Then the great worldwide flood destroyed a world gone astray. Noah was given the rainbow set in the clouds as ensign of the *Noahic*

Covenant in the most common colours seen by the naked eye: Red, Orange, Yellow, Green, Blue, Indigo, and Violet [as listed by Isaac Newton, in English, a popular way of remembering these colours was to memorize the name "ROY G. BIV."]. Like a wheel within a wheel (half a wheel within half a wheel to the human eye given the global characteristic of the earth) as a symbol between God's glory and every living creature for generations in perpetuity

When the anger had subsided the Almighty made a personal promise:

> "While the earth remains, seed time and harvest, cold and heat,
>
> winter and summer, and day and night shall not cease..."

Then Noah was blessed to be fruitful and to multiply as his progeny scattered across the whole face of the earth. The *Noahic covenant* borders with the *Abrahamic Covenant,* spans all succeeding ages, and continues in force despite successive covenants to introduce new administrations.

CHAPTER 2

ABRAHAMIC COVENANT

ABRAM EMERGES AFTER THREE AGES of disappointment in the human race. God tells Abram that at some point he would move to a land he would be directed, conditional on spiritual improvement. The promise related to *blood* and *land* and was to remain in force to be administered by future specific blood covenants. Since then Israel was the vassal of God's land and no other people in the history of mankind have been so preoccupied as the Israelite with the land in which they live. Violation of religious and spiritual obligations continually repeated resulted in the loss of land as punishment for breaking of covenant. When defiled the land `spews' out its inhabitants. On most of the covenants relating to land, the Israelite understood to mean unconditional but later by a succession of foreign conquests of the land it proved not to be so.

Un-Godly acts and bloodshed pollutes and defiles the land, dating back to Cain and Abel. Cain's offer to God was the fruits of his gardening labours and Abel's was the firstlings of his flock. By God's preference to Abel's gift, Cain became jealous of his brother and killed him. God confronted Cain that his brother's blood cried from the ground, for blood is the currency of the spiritual realm. Yet, God forewarned that whosoever caused the death of Cain, punishment would be imposed on him sevenfold. God wanted to punish Cain who took his punishment in the land of Nod, a place of penitence; and that God alone could mete out punishment.

In Abram's time the people were steeped in idolatry and the race was to be revived through him and his descendants to play specific roles to be the thread of the promise of redemption. Abram tried to convince his father, Terach, of the folly of worshipping idols. When he was left alone Abram took a stick and smashed all the idols and placed the stick in the hand of the biggest idol. On his father's return Abram tells him that the big idol got angry and smashed the little ones!

****

EGYPT'S DOMINATION OF SOUTHERN Canaan has waned, the Hebrew race has been a unit until now when God tells Abram to leave his father's house, and proceed to another *Land*. Though separation is inevitable in all its heart-rending forms, most importantly Abram's move strengthens his separation from idolatry. He leads his followers from Ur to Canaan with no fixed abode, they live in mobile dwellings known as tabernacle (tent). Intrinsic in this promise is the inner chamber of a tabernacle, before the 'temporal' *tabernacle* which was a mobile temple as a replica of the heavenly one given to the Jewish nation as bearer symbolic to the human body:

> *"Do you not know that your body is the temple...from God...and you are not your own?"* (1 Corinthians 6:19-20.)

The purpose of the tabernacle was for the ages of ODOM and the identity of the central figure through the Ages is hidden pending his coming as a Redeemer for the whole of mankind.

****

DURING THE WAR BETWEEN a number of ancient city-states in Canaan and Mesopotamia, Abram's nephew Lot, his family and goods had been captured and carted off. Armed with three hundred and eighteen men Abram pursued the invaders, rescued Lot and his family and returned them safely to the Canaanite cities. On Abram's return a mysterious man bursts upon the scene and ministers and blesses Abraham. He is Melchizedek, the king of Salem. When Abram enters the land of Canaan around 2000 BC the city of Jerusalem is called Salem, meaning peace. Unknown at this time Melchizedek was to reappear in the last era of ODOM to minister and bless the *lead player* of the *New Covenant,* in the *tabernacle* yet to be manifested.

****

THE BEGETTING OF AN HEIR is important that Sarai, the barren wife of Abram, shares his sadness and offers her Egyptian handmaid, Hagar to her husband. Since the dawn of time barriers of rank have separated people but individuals are brought into this world under a variety of circumstances some which disregard barriers of rank. Hagar is blessed with the *Maternal Covenant,* and a son is born out of the union of Abram and Hagar and the baby is named Ishmael meaning 'God hears' because God hears Hagar's prayers before she is invited back into Abram's household after she had been banished. Abram is ninety-nine years and God promises that Sarai shall have a son who shall be called Isaac. Abram and Sarai were both advanced in age and were sceptical of this promise.

In Scriptures *Hebrew* means Heber which is the name as Eber, meaning: 'beyond' or from the other side as having crossed over. However, Abram means 'father is exalted' and he is eighth generation from Shem, the eldest son of Noah. God changes the name Abram to *Abraham* and Sarai to *Sarah*.

Abraham is famous for his kindness and hospitality with an uncompromising drive to improve the world.

The line of Abraham's obedience perpetuated by his progeny in response to God's will is continued by the *twelve* who were to be revealed in the *New Covenant.*. The nation Israel was to become a witness to all other nations for the blessing of serving the *one true God* and to expect the promised *lead player* as portrayed by the *tabernacle* yet to manifest.

Sarah is blessed with the *Maternal Covenant* and a son was born to them in advanced years, whom they named Isaac. God promised that Sarah shall be mother of many nations and she became co-ruler with her husband. Abraham was faced with the most difficult test of his faith when he was commanded to sacrifice Isaac who was over twenty as a blood burnt offering for God. Abram built an altar in the mountains of Moriah, placed wood upon it, bound Isaac and laid him upon the wood. The practice was known in the Jewish tradition as the 'Akeidah' meaning 'binding' because Isaac was literally bound on the altar. At the last moment an angel appeared to halt the sacrifice.

Isaac's own faith was tested since he knew that he was to be sacrificed but he accepted the situation like a lamb to the slaughter. The incident strengthens the bond between father and son in their unified dedication of their faith to the *one true God*. Most importantly, the sacrifice of Isaac symbolised two things: the making of the *first altar* as the origin of an altar on the meaning of the `Veil' that will separate a `temporal place' and an `eternal place` of a tabernacle yet to be revealed. The second symbol is the slaughter of the final lamb yet to be revealed, a blood sacrifice as the *way* to the eternal place in a new Passover for the whole of mankind.

The *Abrahamic covenant* is confirmed to both Isaac, son of Abraham and Sarah, and later to their grandson Jacob, son of Isaac and Rebekah.

****

GOD CALLS THE DESCENDANTS OF SHEM to form a separate people. Youngest son of Noah Shem was great grand father of Abraham, and father of all Semites. Jacob, the grandson of Abraham, twin brother of Esau, and his mother Rebekah deceived his blind father, Isaac into giving his blessing to Jacob, a blessing intended for Esau. The latter wanted to kill his brother and Rebekah sent Jacob far away to Haran to stay with her brother Leban. A short stay that lasts for twenty years. Jacob worked for Leban for seven years and he fell in love with the latter's daughter Rachel. On the night of their wedding, as brides are veiled from head to toe, Rachel was substituted for Leah, Rachel's older sister as older daughters must marry first.

Then Jacob works for another seven years and takes Rachel for second wife, theirs is a polygamous society, as Jacob also has two concubines, servants of Leah and Rachel. All the women bear him thirteen children: Rachel has Yosef and Benjamin - Ephraim and Manasseh (the two sons of Yosef) were adopted by their grandfather Jacob to share in his inheritance as his sons; Levi, Issachar, Judah, Jebulon, Simeon, Reuben and a daughter, Dinah by his wife Leah; Dan and Naphtali by Bilhah (Rachel's servant); Gad and Asher by Zilpah (Leah's servant). The children of Jacob are *chosen* and cast in adult life to play key roles in the making and service of the *tabernacle*. Jacob means `usurper' or `deceiver' and God renames him *Israel*, meaning `he struggles with God', Jacob establishes the nation *Israel* and the people become *Israelite*. Jacob Israel is named Levi by his mother Leah and he becomes the first Levi, who is founder of the `Levite' group of Priests that are later cast in the role of performing prayers in the *tabernacle*. Each of Jacob's sons is one of the twelve tribes on whom the tribes are named. Yosef is excluded by his absence through the enslavement into Egypt by his brothers.

The role of the Levites (who never inherit a territory for themselves), along with the other tribes by participation, was devotion to the sacred service in spiritual leadership, known as *Kohen* meaning `to serve' as they are called to direct themselves and others in the proper service to the *one true God*. Kohath is one of the sons of Levi and is the patriarchal founder of the Kohathites, one of the four main divisions of the Levites. He passes on the priestly functions of the Levites by oral testimony to Amram father of Moshe.

****

YOSEF IS THEIR FATHER'S favourite as the much loved son and his father makes for him a tunic in many colours. The other brothers are jealous of him and they sell him into slavery in Egypt. They take the tunic smeared with goat's blood to their father saying they found the tunic and Yosef had disappeared. By his ability to interpret visions and dreams of the Egyptian Pharaoh Sanusret II, Yosef has a strong bond with the Pharaoh. He rises to power as governor and second most powerful man in Egypt.

In Canaan, home of the Hebrew, the famine has driven out Yosef's father, Israel, brothers and members of their family - *spewed out by the land* - they seek refuge in Goshen, Egypt. Yosef recognises his brothers but they do not recognise him. The Pharaoh welcomes them through Yosef and agrees that they work the land and give him one fourth of the harvest. Israel dies and Yosef forgives his brothers for selling him into slavery and takes an oath from them that after his death his bones shall be carried from Egypt to Canaan for burial.

In Egypt the Israelite multiply in abundance and become strong. Before Yosef dies at age one hundred and ten he sees three generations from his two grandsons, Manasseh and Ephraim to whom he passes on the oral testimony of Abraham that God will lead the Israelites back to the land of Canaan and that it shall be the land of the Israelite.

The era of *Genesis* has passed with the passing of the generation of Yosef and that of his friend the Pharaoh, who became Pharaoh Ramesses. He does not know Yosef and his generation. Ramesses and Egypt are in dread of the power of the Israelite and plot against them as they serve with rigour in bondage as slaves of Pharaoh.

CHAPTER 3

EGYP'S NEW PHARAOH

EGYPT'S NEW PHARAOH issues an order to the Hebrew midwives Shiphrah and Puah to kill all newborn Hebrew sons. In the midst of this awesome order Yochebed gives birth to a son and hides him for three months. She is wife of Amram, who had taken her, the sister of his father, for wife, a common practice to give the older women a chance of marriage. They are of the Levi tribe of the Hebrew and have two other children, Miriam and Aaron.

With a heavy heart, such as a mother's heart, Yochebed puts her baby in a wicker basket, secured by slime and pitch, to prevent sinking, and places the basket among the reeds on the bank of the River Nile, with a prayer for the baby to be saved. She then places a great responsibility upon little Miriam to watch over the Basket. Miriam hides in the bulrushes of the Nile as *guardian of the vessel*.

Surrounded by her handmaids Hatshepsut, the Pharaoh's haughty beautiful daughter, is bathing along the river bank close by. She is disturbed by a baby crying. One of her handmaids investigates and finds a basket floating around among the leaves, picks up the basket and brings it to the princess. Hatshepsut looks in the basket, there is a baby as he cries out with strong lungs and kicking all fours for attention. Her heart melts, filled with glee she resolves to keep him as her son, and names him Moshe meaning `drew out' of the water in Egyptian. When it becomes clear that the princess wants to keep the baby, the patient little Miriam, trembling with fear, bravely but cautiously emerges from the bulrushes, approaches the princess and asks if she would like a Hebrew midwife to nurse the baby. The delighted Hatshepsut agrees and the little girl calls a Hebrew woman who becomes Moshe's paid nanny. Yoshebed dare not show her joy and disbelief that her baby is not to be parted from her after all but his true identity must be a kept secret. Moshe was to be raised in the Egyptian royal palace.

Moshe learns the princely Egyptian ways from his adoptive mother Hatshepsut. Yochebed raised him in the humble Godly ways of the Hebrew, and she has a great influence on his life. He grows up in the combination of two cultures with perfect ease as any child would. Moshe as a prince of the realm he gets the best of everything: learning Egyptian science, geography, history, grammar, writing, literature, philosophy, music, and all the wisdom of the Egyptians. By his charisma and intelligence he is most pleasing to Pharaoh and the entire Egyptian court. As a prince he moves in a chariot with guards and all that bedecks the royal life. Among contemporary societies, Egypt is one of the most academic and scientific, if not the most.

The irony is that Moshe is receiving his education in a princely life at the Egyptian royal court, his entire well-being and existence are conducted at the expense of the Pharaoh, the cruel persecutor of his people, the Hebrew. The Hebrew are in the trial of poverty and wander in hunger, cold and scanty clothing, some garbed in sheep skins and goat skins; in the natural habitat of dens and caves of the earth. In the clay of the brick kilns they are supervised by the Egyptian task-master's whip. The living conditions of the poor brick-making Hebrews are in grave contrast to the palaces of the Pharaohs. In the building of the cities of Pithon and Ramases, the Hebrew are in mortar, in brick, and in all manner of service in the field. His siblings Aaron and Miriam are with their kinsmen in Goshen on the eastern border-land of Egypt. The haughty daughter of the Pharaoh, the rich sons of Egypt look down upon the poor, enslaved oppressed Hebrew.

Time has passed and Moshe is now forty. Yochebed is ailing and blind, she is troubled about the secret she has held for so long. She decides to tell Moshe of the circumstances of his birth and the truth of his identity. Moshe is confused and does not know where he belongs but realises that the nanny who so loved, cared for him and on whom he was so dependent upon and loved was his real mother. In the revelation of his true identity he begins to see things differently. At some point Moshe sees an Egyptian slave supervisor beating a Hebrew man and in a rage he kills and buries the Egyptian. It was a natural instinct and a spontaneous act in killing an enemy to protect a Hebrew. On hearing the story Pharaoh realises that Moshe might be a threat to his leadership and seeks to eliminate him.

Moshe goes from prince to pauper and into hiding in the desert, becomes a sheep herder in Midian and in privacy is brought forth into hard times. Midian is a territory east of the Dead Sea and the Jordan River and includes a large part of the Sinai desert. Perhaps unknown even to himself Moshe is preparing for an important leading role. Still unknown to him in the continuation of the human drama he is cast in the role as fthe foremost player in the construction of a *tabernacle* yet unknown.

Miriam and Aaron are still with their kinsmen in Goshen. Aaron marries Elisheba, daughter of Amminadab and the sister of Naashon. They have four children: Nadab, Abihu, Elezar and Ithamar. Miriam is a prophet, a songster and has devoted her life to religious service and has a deep faith in God. On a certain day the herders are clamouring to draw water from the only one and much used well around the Midian desert. Zapporah and her six sisters are pushed in the queue as they are trying to fill their troughs each day for their father's flock. Along comes a dashing young man, he scares off the male shepherds and the sisters get their water. On arrival home Jethro, their father, a Midianite priest is surprised to see them back so early. They tell him they were rescued from the shepherds by a handsome Egyptian who drew enough water for them and watered the flock. Jethro asks why they did not invite him home for some bread. They fetch him and Jethro meets Moshe.

The Jethro family are Midianites from Midian, one of six sons of Abraham by his concubine Keturah who came from a sect of Ethiopians. Their sons are Zimran, Yaqtan, the latter becomes the ancestor of most Arabs. Moshe settles in Jethro's establishment and Zipporah as the eldest is picked for him to marry, in a culture of arranged marriages where the oldest gets the priority of marriage. Born out of the union of Moshe and Zipporah is a son whom Moshe names Gershom meaning 'foreigner' suggestive of his feelings in a foreign land.

Tending a flock of sheep of his father-in-law Moshe leads the sheep in the desert and comes to Horeb the mountain of God, where an angel of God appears to him in a flame of fire from the midst of a bush. He is curious as to the reason the bush is burning without a kindling fire nor does it burn away. Then he hears from the midst of the bush his name called:

> *"Moshe, Moshe!" The voice continues:*
> *"I am the God of your father, the God of Abraham, Isaac and Jacob".*

The voice continues saying God has seen the oppression of God's people by the taskmasters of Egypt; he must lead them out of the land of the Egyptians to a land flowing with milk and honey, the place of the Canaanites and Hittites, Amorites, Perizzites, Hivites and Jebusites. Moshe asks:

> *"What am I that I should go to Pharaoh and free the Israelite, how do I convince them?"*
> *"Tell them I am who I am and that I am has sent you. My name is forever and this is my memorial to all generations."*

The voice assures Moshe that God will be with him all the way, he is not to be afraid, and directs him to see Pharaoh in peace and ask for the freedom of the Israelite so that they may freely worship their one true God. The Egyptians worship idols. Moshe seeks permission from Jethro to return to Egypt and also to take his wife and child, permission is granted and they set out for Egypt. At some point they are joined by Miriam and Aaron who accompany them to Egypt. In Egypt Moshe seeks to see Pharaoh and is re-admitted to the royal court of Egypt for a hearing before Pharaoh with Miriam and Aaron by his side giving him moral support. He makes a peaceful request for the Israelites to be freed. Pharaoh adamantly refuses. The Egyptians cling to the Israelite so they would not have to do their manual work.

Pharaoh tells the taskmaster not to supply straw for bricks to the Israelite but let them get it themselves, all designed to increase their task. The Israelite complain how are they to provide the quote of bricks which they are expected to make. By the Pharaoh's adamant refusal God warns of ten plagues to come against the

Egyptians and gives Moshe directions along with a `staff' for Moshe and a `rod' for Aaron. The plagues descend upon Egypt and in between each plague Moshe makes a demand to Pharaoh to free the Egyptians. For each of the plagues Pharaoh's sorcerers follow suit with their magic and Pharaoh refuses to let the Israelite go.

Then the final plague comes. God's message to Moshe is that each household must select a perfect year old male lamb from the flock and small households are to join larger ones. The lamb is to be slain on the fourteenth day of Abib(the first month in the Jewish calendar, March Spring Equinox in the Roman calendar) at twilight and its blood is to be splashed on the sides and top of their door frames. The blood is a sign on the houses of the Israelite for the angel of death to *pass over* them so that they are protected from the angel of death. At midnight of that day the angel of death passes throughout Egypt at which time every first born from the Pharaoh's son to the son of the slave including the first-born of the cattle are slain.

Pharaoh sends for Moshe and tells him the Israelite are free and he is deported from Egypt. While the Israelite are still in Egypt Moshe and Aaron specifically receives instructions to remember the *Passover* each year for generations to come, and celebrate the event as a special festival for God; and to commemorate the event of their freedom from Egyptian bondage:

> *"Remember this day when you went out of Egypt, out of the house of bondage: for by strength of the hand of the Lord brought you out of this place. No leavened bread shall be eaten"*

CHAPTER 4

Exodus

MOSHE AND AARON round up the community, men, women and children numbering almost a million and hurriedly they leave at night. It is during Egypt's Eighteenth Dynasty as they come out of bondage from Egypt and this is the most significant moment in their history: Egyptian bondage has ended and the era of *Exodus* begins. Moshe, Aaron and Miriam emerge and are cast as the leading figures among the Israelite at the pivotal time of the history of the human drama in search of the *Promised Land.* Going out of Egypt without a backward glance they cannot take much with them, travellers with no fixed home, parents carrying loads of basic needs for daily existence for all, towering above heads of little children tottering behind not to lose sight of the rest of the family. The older ones minding the little ones, taking their little hands, as parents are `all hands on'. In addition to their load Moshe and other men take the bones of Yosef and of his brothers to honour the oath made in Egypt. Pharaoh realises Egypt has lost the services of the Israelite by letting them go and the men of the Egyptian army pursue them headed by Pharaoh mounted on a horse. Unwavering Moshe assures the people that God is with them and the Red Sea becomes dry ground as they cross it but the waters crash down upon Pharaoh and horse and the pursuing Egyptian solders. Miriam is the songster who leads the people into songs of worship, singing, dancing and playing the tambourines and drums.

As they cross the Red Sea they sing one of the most well-known of ten songs of redemption, *Shirat Ha Yam* (*Song of the Sea),* in praise of God for the miraculous redemption out of Egypt:

> "I will sing to the Lord, for he is highly exalted.
> he has triumphed gloriously...
> The horse and its rider he has hurled into the sea...

The Lord shall reign forever and ever..."

They follow a pillar of cloud by day, and at night the pillar of cloud is replaced by a pillar of fire, another common descriptor of God's appearance to light the way; so as they travel by day and night, guided step by step on their way to the *Promised Land*. They are nourished from Goshen to the wilderness of Sinai for about fifty days as they shuffle through the Sinai desert sand.

The Sinai is very diverse, wide open plains and high sand dunes, sandstone hills and rocks shaped by winds, green oases but in hidden canyons. Once a sea, the desert is now a shell of sand as the sea lives on in the sand, as its particular destiny, and may continue till water covers it up again. The desert, like everything else on earth, foliage, minerals, and such as adorns the earth has its own destiny to fulfil. The towering brilliant but distant moon above pales the stars, the darkest hour of the night will come just before dawn, the bitterest point of nocturnal cold, only the sound of the eternal wind constantly changing the dunes, the horizons so distant. Henceforth the bondage lift is the *First Passover* that has set the Israelite free. They cannot go back, the past is unimportant and their concern is only about the best way forward.

It is not all smooth shuffling as they are beset with many problems. Most of the people feel lost not in terms of the way forward but overcome by their own fear of death arising out of their lack of faith in Moshe and in a God they know not, idol worshippers such as they have been. The fear of suffering is worse than the suffering itself. They blame Moshe for taking them out of Egypt and from an existence they felt to be more acceptable than where they were presently at, heading for an unknown destination. There was also discontentment in Aaron and Miriam as they question and challenge Moshe's authority since he was the only one who was receiving God's directions.

When the Israelite come to the Wilderness of Sin, somewhere between Elim and Sinai on the fifteenth day of the second month after they left the land of Egypt, they start to grumble about hunger. God promises Moshe that the heavens will rain food to the ground. Next morning as the people wake up and look around they see little white flakes all around the camp. They ask: *What is it?* The answer is *manhu* in Hebrew, hence *manna* [from heaven]. They eat the manna as bread and all around are birds in abundance, they catch and roast them.

Taught by oral testimony Moshe alone believes in the promise made to Abraham, he is confident in the truthfulness of the God of Jacob, and, therefore, chooses rather to suffer affliction with the people as he forges on. He continues to impress upon the people of the truth in one God as he leads them towards the *Promised Land.* They set up their tents and camp in front of Mount Sinai, like Abraham and his group in their time living in tents.

Moshe goes alone to Mount Sinai and God speaks and confirms with Moshe the *Mosaic Covenant* initially made at Horeb. The covenant is made between God and the nation Israel through Moshe as their chosen leader. The period of the *Abrahamic covenant* has ended with the rashly acceptance of the *Mosaic Covenant* at Sinai exchanging the tenets of *grace* for *law.* Moshe receives two stone tablets on which inscribed are the *Ten Commandments*; directing how fallen humans ought to live in order to glorify the Creator; it underlines all covenants; and applies to all saved and unsaved humans of every era, to be judged according to their response to it, in degrees of acts and punishment. The *Sabbath* is confirmed in the *Fourth Commandment* as the ensign of the *Mosaic covenant,* the covenant is also known as the *Old*

Covenant. In observation of the completion of God's perfect work the *Passover* is to be part and parcel of the covenant; and the moral law shows fallen humans in their condemned condition and the need for God's redemptive grace.

The fourth ODOM made with Abraham also ends when Moshe provides a sacrifice for the guilty and by divine power that has brought the Israelite out of bondage. Moshe remains at Sinai for forty days where God continues to give him directions for the Israelite including civil and ceremonial laws for their worship and daily living.

Moshe is in his eighty-first year as God directs him to construct a *tabernacle* and to tell the people of Israel to make a contribution for the making of the *tabernacle, a* `tent of meeting', as a sanctuary; and an *Ark of Covenant.* All, according to their willingness and ability, so that God may dwell among them. After the forty days Moshe returns from Mount Sinai with the two stone tablets of the *Ten Commandments* and finds the people have gone back to their old ways and he is deeply angered. Under Aaron's instructions they made offerings of gold and built an idol in the shape of a golden calf and they bowed to worship it. The *Fifth Commandment* of the *Ten Commandments* specifically prohibits the worship of idols.

Moshe follows God's wish and gathers together the people and tells them that God has asked them to make a contribution according to their willingness and ability towards the building of a *tabernacle*. Their contribution is to be gold, silver, bronze; yarn in blue, purple and scarlet; fine linen; goat's hair, rams' skins dyed red and hides of sea cows; badger skins, acacia wood; olive oil for lighting; spices and oil for anointing and fragrant incense; and onyx stones and other gems to be mounted on the ephod and breastplate depicting the twelve tribes of Israel. The work is to be done in six days and on the seventh day, a holy Sabbath, is to be a day of rest and no fire is to be kindled in any of their dwellings – a replica of God's Creation in six days, expressed as a visible object: the *tabernacle.*

To each of the twelve tribes an area is allocated where they construct their dwelling tents in an orderly fashion; with their families, each son as head of his family behind the yet to be made *tabernacle*: eastward, westward, northward and southward; and circling an area reserved for the *tabernacle*. The Aaronanites: Moshe, Aaron and Miriam as the descendants of Kohath, second son of Levi, camp on the eastward side front and centre area of prominence so that they face west where the *tabernacle* is to be; also on the same side are Judah, Issachar and Zebulun. On the westward side are the Gershonites: Benjamin, Ephraim and Manasseh. Northward side are Merarites: Dan, Asher and Naphtali. On the Southward side are the Kohathites: Gad, Simeon and Reuben.

One year has passed since the Israelite left Egypt. On the first day of the first month of the second year Moshe receives orders to set up the *tabernacle*. The era of *Leviticus* in the rules for Levite priests begins. He picks Bezalel son of Uri and grandson of Hur of the tribe of Judah as skilful in various crafts; also Oholiath son of Achisamach of the tribe of Dan as one with the ability to teach others the necessary skills. The pupils have been filled with the skills of craftsmen, weavers and master designers. Miriam has assembled all the women who are gifted to design, embroider and weave fine linen and make yarn and those gifted have spun yarn of goat's hair.

The people bring to Moshe their completed gifts, all the materials and components required and Moshe blesses them and passes the materials to the working team from the generosity of the people, and the wealthy have donated the gem stones for the ephod and breastplate. The *Aaronic Priestly Covenant* is granted through his brother Moshe to Aaron and his descendants in which are described glorious adornments of sacred vestments. The *Covenant* is perpetual establishing a ministerial priesthood outlining its obligations; for as long as the heavens endure, that he should preside over worship, act as priest, and bless the people in the name of YAHWEH.

AARON IS THE CHOSEN ONE to offer sacrifices of incense and perfume as a memorial to make amends for the people. Aaron and his sons direct all the various services to be performed by the Gershonites and Eleazar, the son of Aaron, is the overall supervisor of the leaders that are assigned the various duties of the sanctuary.

Special duties are given to each of three priestly lines, sons of Levi: Gershon, Kohath and Merari. Each item is assigned individually, fixing the sockets, rearing up the pillars and bars by hand, and putting in place all that is required.

The duty is assigned to the Gershonites for assembling and dismantling the tabernacle covers, curtains, screens and cords of the `tent of meeting', the *tabernacle*; and its covering, the covering of the skin of small whale (porpoise) at the top; for the tent of meeting: the screen for the doorway, its covering; for the court of the tent: the hangings and the screen for the doorway which is around the *tabernacle;* and the altar and its cords.

The Kohathites are appointed custodians of the holy objects: including the carrying of them along their travels: the *Ark of Covenant*, the lamp-stand, altars with poles; the table; the utensils of the sanctuary for ministering; the screen and all the relevant items for the prayer service. The duty of carrying other items from one place to another is assigned to the sons of Merari, under the direction of Ithamar the son of Aaron. But to the sons of Kohath, he confines their service to the holy objects, which only the Kohathites are to hand carry or shoulder the load.

CHAPTER 5

THE SINAI DESERT

THE TABERNACLE IS TO CONSIST of three areas: The outer court, the *Courtyard;* The inner court, the *Holy Place;* and the inner most, the *Holy of Holies.* Every item of materials used in the construction bears a symbolic meaning and the focus is on sacrifice, judgment, cleansing and representing the Ages of ODOM. The Courtyard representing the *Mosaic Law* and measures a volume of 1500 cubits, represented one thousand five hundred years of the time or span of the *Mosaic Law* was to be in force. The Courtyard was the place where the shewbread, lamp stand (candlestick – Menorah) and the Altar of Incense were to be kept.

Description of the Courtyard, where animals were to be sacrificed for the forgiveness of sin:

150ft long x 75ft wide [feet are used for easy reading].

Surrounded by fine linen, 7.5ft high (lea – unit of measure of linen). Supportive post in sockets of Bronze – symbol of judgement of sin.

There is only one entrance through a Gate of 30ft wide, located to the east and one faces the west at entry to the Tabernacle.

Items in the Courtyard:

    a) The brazen Altar
       Size - 7.5ft x 7.5ft x 7.5ft
       Material – Acacia Wood covered with metal (brass, bronze or copper signify the *judgment of God*)
       Offerings – animal sacrifices burning day or night for the forgiveness of sins.
    b) Laver (wash basin) of cleansing:

No description of the pattern or shape of the container given but it holds water and sits on a base, and it is placed between the door of the Holy Place and the altar (the priest first makes sacrifice for himself before he comes to the altar (God is approached by blood and water).

Before the priests enter into the Holy Place, they have to wash their hands and feet at the laver.

The *Fence* is tent-like and is made of fine white linen symbolising *righteousness*; with hangings of the hair of goat and ram for apology or atonement; held by 60 pillars of acacia wood, denoting the *humanity of a Redeemer* yet to come - 10 pillars on the east and west and 20 pillars on the north and south; each pillar has an ornamental band of silver on top; the boards are overlaid with gold representing *Deity;* and fitted together to form walls of 45 feet by 15 feet. The upright pillars are each set into a socket within a bronze base; they are 5 cubits high and 5 cubits apart, passing from pillar to pillar is a rod and upon these are silver hooks from which hang the linen; silver denotes *ransom. The w*eaving of Cherubim around the linen fabric of the *Fence* emphasises the righteousness of God and of those who serve in holiness. Without the Fence at the entry gate there is an altar in brass, and as for bronze, symbolises the *Place of Judgment* where the repentant will seek blood sacrifice.

The Tabernacle:

> 45ft long x 15ft high x 15ft wide
> This contains a first chamber called *The Holy Place* and a further inner chamber called the *Holy of Holies*. These two places are separated by a *Veil*.
> This whole unit has the following:
> Underneath – Acacia Wood (*humanity / man*)
> Covered in Gold (*deity / God*)

Boards set in socket of Silver (ransom) -
The silver is in the socket where the boards are set in place – this being in the foundation of the tabernacle.
Hence God's redemption is set on a firm foundation.
There are 4 layers over the whole unit.

The 4 layers are:

    a)   1st Outermost covering – skin which is waterproof
    b)   2nd layer – Ram skin dyed red
    c)   3rd layer – Goat skin
    d)   4th layer – White linen embroidered with Purple, White, Red and Blue.

The *Holy Place* (1st chamber), symbolising the human body on its temporal earthly sojourn as a temple housing the spirit:

> 30ft long x 15ft high x 15ft wide (entry from the *Courtyard* is through a curtain into the *Holy Place*).
> 3 articles contained in this place:
> (i)   North side – The Table of Shewbread – *twelve* loaves displayed in the *Holy Place* symbolises the *Redeemer* who has come as the *Bread of Life,* as the *Way* and Salvation is *Justification;* and *Twelve also* stand for the twelve Disciples chosen by Yeshua and symbolising the twelve tribes of Israel.
> (ii)   South side – The Golden 7 Branch Candlestick (also known as *Golden Menorah*), the Lamp Stand made of pure gold. In the socket is silver where the boards are set in place - this being in the foundation of the tabernacle.

Hence God's redemption is set on a firm foundation. Oil for the lamp and incense symbolises the *Holy Spirit*.

West side – Altar of Incense symbolises the *Redeemer* as the *Intercessor*.

The *Holy Place* in the Ages of Dispensation represents *Grace* and its area measurement is equal to two thousand years of a `Church Age and Truth of a Redeemer yet to come' and the aspect of Salvation in earthly present Age is *Sanctification;* a place for humans in their un-glorified state and is under the ceremonial law and sanctuary subject to the *Ten Commandments*. Only the priests may enter the *Holy Place* and then when fully cleansed.

The *Lamp Stand* is made of gold and silver, the gold symbolising the *Redeemer as the Light of the World*; and silver denotes redemption.

(iii)   The *Holy of Holies* (2nd chamber), symbolic to the spirit:

15ft long x 15ft high x 15ft wide – perfect cube, The Trinity. The width is 45ft (total) - 30ft (1st chamber) = 15ft It contains the Ark of Covenant. Between the 1st chamber and the 2nd chamber is a Veil, of the same four colours of the whole unit; and symbolises the body of a Redeemer

yet to come as the Way through the Veil - as the blood of the lamb at Habib was the object of the Passover to save the Israelite from the angel of death, so too is Yeshua the Passover through the barrier, the Veil, that had kept people from the presence of God.

The *Veil* is woven in a linen fabric of blue, symbolising heavens or heavenly nature; in a thread of purple, signifying kingly or royalty, and scarlet, denoting blood sacrifice; with an artistic design of Cherubim associated with the holiness of God and the righteous government of the Almighty. The *Holy of Holies* is the everlasting 'heavenly place' in its Ages of Dispensation and is a *Messianic Kingdom yet* to come, representing one thousand years of the rule of the *Messianic-Redeemer* as the *Life* and the aspect of *Salvation* in *Glorification*.

The Ark of Covenant:

a) The Ark is a box consisting of a rectangular chest made of acacia wood and measures 31 x 9" long and 2' x 3" width and height; and it is overlaid with pure gold, inside and outside, with a moulding (or crown) of gold around its top.
b) On the bottom of the box, are four rings of gold casting and are attached (fixed in place) to the feet of the ark on which two poles, also made of wood are affixed.

The *Ark of Covenant* dwells in the *Holy of Holies,* shielded from view, and is in two parts: the Ark, also known as the *Ark of*

Testimony and *Mercy Seat*, an atonement cover, on the top of the Ark. Undoubtedly this is the most fascinating holy piece of furniture ever made. Spiritually, the Ark is the manifestation of God's physical presence on earth: the *Shekinah,* literally meaning `caused to dwell' signifying that it is a divine visitation or presence of YAHWEH on earth.

The Mercy Seat:

a) The Mercy Seat is made of pure gold overlaid with gold, a kind of lid closing the chest from above, made of wood held in place by a ridge or crown.
b) On the top of the Mercy Seat are two cherubim, celestial angelic beings in the Spiritual Realm, and they are made of gold, one at each end, and their wings spread over the mercy seat, as shielding the top of the seat.
The Cherubim are the executors of God's righteous and holy judgment.
c) Two poles made of acacia wood and overlaid with gold, are to remain in the rings but not generally believed to be fixed into position.

The two cherubim in the *Spiritual Realm*, their wings spread over the *Mercy Seat* over the *Ark of Covenant* indicate that in redemption *Mercy overrules Judgment.*

The *Shekinah,* a cloudy pillar, first appears when the Israelite set out from Succoth in their escape from Egypt, in the day and a fiery pillar by night. Whenever Moshe enters the tent, a pillar of cloud descends and settles at the entrance of the tent of meeting between the two Cherubim under the cover of a glowing cloud where God speaks to Moshe. His relationship between the Ark and the *Shekinah* is to be reinforced by the recurring motif of clouds - God's presence in the guise of a cloud.

Moshe as directed asks the Israelite to give him twelve staffs from each of their ancestral tribes with the name of each head written on his staff. The purpose was that the staff that `sprouts' was God's chosen overall leading priest. When Moshe enters the tent the following morning he finds that Aaron's staff has not only sprouted but budded, blossomed and produced almonds; and he places into the Ark three items as directed: the two stone tablets of the *Ten Commandments*, a golden pot of manna, and Aaron's budded staff; and hands back the other staffs to each head of the tribes.

When the High Priest enters in the presence of the Ark he does so only under the cover of a cloud of incense, intended to mask the sight of the *Shekinah* in all glory. The Levites hold a special rank in the duties of the *Tabernacle* and its significance. Kohath passes on the priestly functions of the Levites by oral testimony to his son Amram.

****

MOSHE IS KING IN JESHURUN in hard work and responsibility, truly a remarkable shepherd in more than one sense. In the *Hebrew Bible* a poetic name for Israel meaning upright and just, a description meant for Israel's unwavering stance from the ways and standards set by God for the Israelite.

The era of *Exodus* is passing and they are about to commence the *era of Leviticus* and the beginning of the priesthood in the direction of the Tabernacle. As they move from one place to another the Israelite dismantle the *Tabernacle*, share the load of carrying the separate components to the next camp-site. There they reassemble the components and their dwelling tents. The Leviticus Priesthood vests through the three sons of Levi: Gershon, Kohath, second son of Levi an ancestor of Moshe, and Merari.

Aaron as the first *kohen* and founder of the priestly clan representing kindness, peace and the pursuance of peace, loving fellow man, focussing and invoking life's energies on sanctity and purpose, and invoke heavenly influence. Aaron and his sons Nadab, Abihu, Elezar and Ithamar, have a special place and are the only ones who can offer animal sacrifices or incense. They also bring fellow Levites from their ancestral tribe to join them in performing their duties in the *Holy Place* but the fellows are not sanctioned to enter the *Holy of Holies*.

Now Moshe begins the task of anointing the first priests, Aaron and his sons. Moshe first washes Aaron thoroughly with water and the purpose is to remove his `iniquity' (badness): symbolising that the human body is an *earthly tabernacle or temple* that temporarily houses the spirit and it is essential that the human temple be hygienically clean. When Moshe is preparing Aaron for duties within the inner chamber of the *Holy of Holies*, he puts on Aaron the Ephod. It is made in two parts, front and back; and clasped together at the shoulders with two onyx stones set in gold by a girdle or sash of variegated work. The Ephod is in a boxlike knit, made of turquoise wool and twisted fine linen skilfully and elaborately embroidered in threads of gold, blue, purple and scarlet; it is an outer garment, a kind of apron, over his priestly robe like a tunic. Both Ephod and girdle signify *righteousness.*

On the Ephod are two other stones of onyx on the shoulder-piece with the names of the sons of Israel – six on one stone and six on the other, in the order of their birth engraved on them. Two shoulder straps are fastened to the front of the Ephod by golden rings to which the Hoshen or breastplate is attached by golden chains with straps and ribbons.

The breastplate is made from the same material as the Ephod, embroidered linen, it is square, a cubit in width, two layers thick and with twelve precious engraved jewels in four rows, each embedded upon it, and each jewel framed in gold; chains of gold like braided cords are fastened to the settings. It has a pocket folded to a double, enabling two other stones to be kept on the inside over the heart area. Its function is to form a space in the breastplate for the *Urim* and *Thummim* that denotes `perfect light'. Each of the stones is engraved with the names of the Twelve Tribes of Israel, a branch of Judah, each son is one branch of Israel, six on each shoulder. Aaron is representing all the tribes before God. The Hoshen is a Breastplate of judgement and the purpose of wearing it is atonement for sin of errors in judgement on the children of Israel. Followed by the mitre or turban, a fine piece of linen that was wrapped around the head, colours and materials used are significant to the *tabernacle* and the holy crown or head-plate of gold, engraved: *Kodesh l'Adonai* (*Holiness to Yahweh*) with all its memorial adjuncts of glory and beauty.

The head-plate is made of pure gold and tied with a turquoise blue wool cord, and is with an embroidered sash on the Turban/Mitre. Then the robe of blue, its hem is of alternating bells and pomegranates of turquoise, purple, and scarlet wool - signifying *healing*: the bells for *words* and the pomegranates for *deeds*, combined for his obedient life, followed by his healing for himself and for his fellow priests who are joint partakers. As an under garment, linen Breeches are worn, the length being from the hips to the thighs. Moses consecrates his brother Aaron and anoints him with holy oil. The *Aaronic Covenant*, an everlasting *Covenant* is for Aaron and for his descendants. Moshe has entrusted Aaron with commandments, committed him to the statues of the Law and decrees for Aaron to teach Israel and enlighten him on the law. Aaron is directed that himself, his sons and family are to bear the responsibility for offences connected with the sanctuary for which they have an overall term *tent of meeting* (the *Tabernacle*) and they are to bear the responsibilities connected with the priesthood. Twelve loaves of shewbread are displayed in the *Holy Place* to be renewed every *Sabbath*.

First thing in the morning a number of priests are on duty in the Temple of the *Tabernacle* as they divide into two groups to make a pre-daylight inspection of the Temple courtyard; then they meet and walk in two columns for the assignment of the daily duties. They are selected by lot four times during the day; twice before the gate is opened and twice after. Choosing by lot prevents personal ego from having a part in the selections. A censer full of burning coal is associated with the sweet incense which is put on live coal so the heat causes the incense to create a smoke to shield Aaron from the Ark. The Ark cannot be touched as the consequence would be death of the one touching it. The coals of the previous day's fire remain glowing on the altar of burnt offerings. A priest, chosen by lot, stirs the fire into fresh flame. Then another lot taken to designate those taking part in the sacrifice itself; those in the *Holy Place* who are to trim the wicks of the golden candlestick (*menorah*) and to add oil; and those who are to prepare the altar of incense.

High Priests are appointed by Moshe for life to perform duties in the *Holy of Holies.* Once a year on the Day of Atonement (forgiveness) only one out of the group of High Priests is chosen to enter and serve at the *Holy of Holies*, sanctified and consecrated forever to be in the presence of God. The chosen priest is to be the interceptor or advocate who is regarded sufficiently sanctified to mediate between sinner and God.

Prior to entering the *Holy of Holies* the chosen priest must abstain from marital relations for several days. Before entering the *Holy of Holies* Aaron has slaughtered and offers the blood of a bull as the forgiveness of sins for himself and forgiveness for his household. He takes the blood of the slaughtered bull and finely ground sweet incense, in aromatic botanic material which releases fragrant smoke when burned, through the Veil into the *Holy of the Holies* which he presents before God. The cloud of the incense covers the mercy seat on the *Ark of Covenant*, the top of the chest, and he takes some of the blood of the bull and sprinkles it on the mercy seat and also at the front of the chest.

He also takes through the Veil the blood of a slaughtered goat as an offering for the people and follows the same process as for the blood of the bull. The purpose is an apology for the impurities and transgressions of the Israelite.

No one is to be present in the Tent of Meeting (the outer court of the Tabernacle) from the time Aaron enters the Holy Place until he has made atonement for himself, his household and the entire community of Israel. Two goats are presented to God at the entrance of the Tent of Meeting, outside of the outer court. The cast lots and one goat becomes the sin offering for slaughtering to obtain the blood for sprinkling and the other as the *scapegoat*.

When Aaron has finished atoning for the Holy Place, he goes back into the Tent of Meeting and the altar, then he goes outside of the Tent of Meeting, and outside of the outer court of the Tabernacle, to present the live goat: laying hands on its head, openly confesses sins of the people, literally laying the sins on the head of the goat as he sends it away into the wilderness. The sacrifice under the law of atonement is meant to cover all known and unknown sins, both individual and national are removed and sent away with the scapegoat [hence origin of 'scapegoat' one who is blamed for the wrongdoings, mistakes, or faults of others, especially for reasons of expediency].

Then Aaron offers up two rams required for a burnt offering, one for the *Holy Place* and the other for the community from the smoke of the fat of the animal offering on the Altar in the Tent of Meeting. The bull and the goat of the sin offering whose blood was taken through the Veil are taken outside the camp along with their hides and flesh and all refuse and put into the fire to burn. Those seeking forgiveness of sin come to the *Courtyard* with an animal offering as compensation, hand it over to the priests as *mediators for the present time* to make atonement and intercession on their behalf.

Then Aaron washes his clothes and bathes his body with water, after which he enters the camp. There he makes a burnt offering for the people and makes an apology for himself, his household and for the people. Those who carry out the chores wash their clothes and bathe their bodies with water then enter the camp.

Although God chose them and told them that they needed to depend on the Almighty for their sins to be forgiven; and though individuals chose God, collectively the Israelite did not choose God apparent by their lack of obedience to God and the consequent punishment in the loss of land. Sadly they only performed and followed all the ceremonies as a `ritual' but without any true understanding. They did nothing more than follow instructions, possibly more out of fear of the elders or the priests or both and lied in unbelief. Their memories were short, as they repeatedly became disobedient as shown in the whole of the Old Testament. Hence they were not led straight into the land promised to Abraham. Forty days of spying turned into forty years of wandering in the wilderness due to their unbelief, as a result of which a whole generation had to die in the desert.

The Israelite are now in the *era of Numbers* in the census of counting members of the community. Though Moshe and Aaron are Kohathites by their father's tribe they both hold a special rank in the duties of the *Tabernacle* and its significance. And, due to this service, they are not to be included in the census with the other eleven tribes, a privilege not only exclusive to the Kohathites but to the tribe of Levites as a whole. The years have passed under the leadership of Moshe and as each head of a tribe passes on, the eldest son takes over the name and the responsibilities of the deceased within the community. God has denied Moshe the *Promised Land* by his act of disobedience, contrary to his unquestionable obedience all along. Previously, when God had told Moshe along with Aaron and the people to smite the rock for much needed water Moshe obeyed; but on a subsequent occasion when God instructed him to speak to the rock, he instead smote it twice. This much displeased YAHWEH.

CHAPTER 6

THE ERA OF NUMBERS PASSES

THE ERA OF NUMBERS HAS COME TO PASS and they are now in the *era of Deuteronomy* where Moshe delivers his final three speeches to the Israelite in the plains of Moab, shortly before he dies and before they enter the *Promised Land*. They camped near the town of Suph in the Sinai Desert east of the Jordan River. Earlier Moshe had defeated the Amorite King Sihon of Heshbon. It would have taken them only eleven days to walk from Mount Sinai to Kadesh-Barnea by way of the Mount Seir Road, but these speeches were not made until forty years after they left Egypt.

In the first speech Moshe reviews the forty years of wilderness wanderings which led to this moment and he tells the people that God said they had stayed in Sinai long enough and they should leave the place and go into the land that belongs to the Amorites and their neighbours the Canaanite:

> *"I give you this land, just as I promised your ancestors Abraham, Isaac, and Jacob."*

The land includes Jordan River Vale, the hill country, the western foothills, the Southern Desert, the Mediterranean sea coast, the Lebanon mountains, and all the territory as far as the Euphrates River. Moshe ends by teaching them `his law' and how to observe it. He goes on to say that God had blessed them and Israel was too big for one person: *"There are as many of us as there are stars in the sky."* He could not take care of their problems and settle all their arguments alone. Each tribe was to choose experienced men who were known for their wisdom and he would make them the official leaders of their tribes. He appointed some as leaders, others military officers in charge of groups of varying numbers, a thousand, a hundred, fifty. He also appointed judges and gave them instructions to settle legal cases with fair decisions and to apply the same rules to Israelite and non-Israelite, without regard to the helpless or powerful status of the litigants. They were not to fear anyone and God would help them in making fair decisions. In cases they could not resolve Moshe would be the supreme judge of such decisions.

Then he taught them the Lord's commands. In his second speech he reminded the Israelite of the need for exclusive allegiance to the *one true God* and observance of the laws and the teachings he had given them upon which possession of the *Promised Land* depended. The third speech offers the comfort that even should Israel prove unfaithful so lose the land, with repentance it could be restored. He impresses upon the definitive statement of Jewish identity:

"Hear O Israel: the LORD our God, the LORD is one" - the *one true God* of Abraham. They have wandered around and around in the wilderness, they are almost in sight of the *Promised Land* but Moshe dies and his generation has also passed on. Those left are mostly born during the wilderness years. By this time the Israelite number two million and the year is about 1272 BC. God calls Joshua son of Nun and Moshe's minister and tells him to lead the Israelite on and cross the River Jordan:

> *"Every place on which the soles of your feet will tread I havegiven you...*
> *ollow the Torah that my servant Moshe has commanded you..."*

Moshe was the face of the *sun*, now replaced by Joshua, the face of the *moon*, a reflection of teacher to pupil. Only Joshua and his good friend Caleb are left of the first generation since they departed from the bondage of Egypt. Joshua leads them on carrying the *Tabernacle and the Ark of Covenant* forward in his unshakeable faith. They are about to enter the *Promised Land* and now Joshua is the mouthpiece of YAWEH. He is directed to put into the Ark gems such as silver, gold, bronze, iron and others. The Kohathites using the affixed poles carry on their shoulders the *Ark of Covenant* into the centre of the Jordan River now at a flood stage and the waters miraculously recede, as did the Red Sea waters in the time of Moshe when they left Egypt, they safely cross to dry land. They have travelled for twenty-eight days as they reach the *Promised Land* but the land is bounded by the Egyptian empire to the south and Mesopotamia to the north. Neither of them rules it but seven Canaanite tribes inhabit thirty-one fortified city-scattered areas each under its own king; and the Egyptian Pharaoh has appointed regents in the area.

****

THE ISRAELITE ARE BEYOND THE JORDAN and they establish a communal settlement, at Gilgal. Joshua sends an envoy to the Canaanites claiming the land promised by God to their forefathers and ask the Canaanites to leave peacefully. Things do not go smoothly and they meet with grave opposition. Jericho is the entrance to the heartland of Canaan. The battle begins. They place on the top of the *Ark of Covenant* the *Veil*, the tachash skins (fine leather from sea animals); and a blue cloth on top; concealed even from the Kothahite Levites who carry it. The concealment relates to the absolute holiness of YAHWEH.

The scriptures record that no one can see God and live, therefore anyone who touches the Ark dies, and a temporary dwelling place of YAHWEH among the redeemed manifests as an Almighty presence in their midst. The Kohathite priests shoulder-carry the Ark and holy objects of furniture on poles and bars ahead of armed men.

They continue with the usual custom: the Kohathites are exclusively entrusted with the holy objects; sounding seven trumpets of rams' horns, they circle the walls of Jericho taking six days before they break the walls. They engage in a number of battles resorting to spying and other battle strategies, sometimes victorious but also facing defeat and casualties of their numbers. The spies find refuge in the house of Rahab the harlot. She hides them from the king's forces and they make mutual oaths. She promises that she will not reveal them and they forge an alliance with her. Rahab has an enduring faith in God. The Hebrews conquer the city as they spare Rahab and her family. Fearing imminent defeat by the Hebrews, calling them Habiru, who are taking city after city, Abdi-Heba one of the Canaanite rulers of Jerusalem sends a written appeal to Egyptian Pharaoh Akhenaton; and warns him that his fellow regents in the area are succumbing to the attack of the Habiru and that Zimrida of Lakisi, another Canaanite king, has sided with them.

After conquering Jericho, Joshua leads the Israelite to Schechem, the territory of Yosef's second son Ephraim, to honour the promise made to Yosef that his bones and those of his brothers be buried in the *Promised Land.* They do not set up the tent of meeting in the *Tabernacle* of Moshe, because of the prevailing circumstances and this is the first time the Ark is separated from the Tabernacle. Joshua's Altar is built at Mount Ebal in Schechem and the Ark is placed in the valley between the edges of two mountains, Ebal and Gerzim among a million Israelite.

The Jebusites had built a city which they called `Jebus' with a solid defence wall around the city. The Jebusites are Canaanite descended from Canaan, son of Ham and grandson of Noah; the Amorite are the descendants of the sons of Japhat, Noah's second son, are among those who have been controlling the area and surrounding areas in a succession of power-holding. Joshua has conquered the southern and northern portions of Canaan. He defeats Adoni-zedek, king of Jebus of the Amorites and captures the city of Jebus. With this conquest the area is getting to be known as *Israel.* Joshua continues to maintain the *Tabernacle* and *Ark of Covenant* and in the latter are kept the Ten Commandments, Aaron's rod, a jar of manna, and the first Torah scroll written by Moshe.

After Joshua dies, relatively chaotic years ensue, and the Biblical era of *Kings* follows that of Judges. During the time of Joshua the tribes were unified in faithfulness to YAHWEH and the land rested from war. In the era of the Judges things became different, the people were less unified and were continually at risk from surrounding people doing as they please. There are seven male judges in all, and one woman, Deborah; three minor judges; and Samson was the last judge. Othaniel, the first judge, was the son of Kenaz and brother of Caleb who crossed the River Jordan into

Canaan with Joshua; and five minor judges.

Deborah, a prophetess of God of the Israelite, the fourth Judge of pre-monarchical Israel, counsellor, warrior and the wife of Lapdoth, sings with Barak a victory hymn about the defeat of the adversaries of Israel. Deborah and Barak lead one of the greatest last battles of the Israelite over the northern Canaanite armies in the `Battle of Deborah', defeating the city of Hazor, about thirty years after Joshua first entered Canaan.

There is a social deterioration in the breakdown of religious sensitivity, and inevitable civil war amongst the tribes follows. As a headless society influenced the rise of the monarchy, which was less religious but brought stability to a troubled people. The promise of land to Abraham under the *Abrahamic Covenant* was unconditional and the pledge to remove the inhabiting Jebusites was conditional upon Israel's obedience to the covenant. Joshua and his people had placed the *Ark of the Covenant* at Shiloh, the village in the area settled by the tribes of Benjamin and Ephraim. Shiloh is now known as the *home of the Lord's Tabernacle* where the Israelite bring their sacrifices for the forgiveness of sin. The Ark remains in Shiloh for three hundred and six years.

****

HANNAH, WIFE OF ELIKANAH, resident in Ramathim-Zophim, is barren. Her husband's other wife has children and taunts Hannah, a situation not unlike that of Hagar and Sarah in the days of Abraham. At the temple in Shiloh Hannah is praying intently for a child and makes a promise to God that if she bore a son, she would place him in God's service. Then Eli, a priest at Shiloh, promises Hannah that she is going to bear a son. Hannah is blessed with the *Maternal Covenant*, has a son and names him Samuel, meaning `God hears'. When he is three years old Hannah hands Samuel over to Eli, the high priest at Shiloh, and left to his care for training as a priest in the Shiloh Temple. Hannah and her husband Elikanah return home to Ramathaim-Zophim. Then they have three other sons and two daughters.

Samuel becomes Israel's first prophet dedicated and devoted to God forever and is serving the *Temple* in Shiloh. At Shiloh Eli, the high priest, has two sons. The sons are treating offerings to God with contempt and sexual sin abounds. Although Eli has challenged his sons indicating that he did not approve of their conduct, God rebukes and pronounces judgment on Eli for allowing the continuance of disrespect to God. After Eli's death Samuel becomes a judge of Israel at the age of twenty-two. He was about fifty-five when he prophesied over Saul and anointed him as king.

The era of Judges endures up to the time of Samuel. The Israelite are in a succession of associated sovereignty; intervals of anarchy; and some years referred to as full years in a strong practice of idolatry. The worst is the worship of Baal (baalim plural) meaning `lord' a supreme god of ancient Canaan and Phoenicia and widespread in Canaan in the era of the Judges. For some time the Philistines had been extending their rule over large parts of Canaan. The Ark is still at Shiloh until the time of the Philistines, a seafaring non-Semitic people who have left Crete and arrived in Canaan.

The Philistines are the Descendants of Casluchim, who was descendant of Mizraim, son of Ham, one of the three sons of Noah, they inhabit the Mediterranean coast of Canaan. Israel went out to battle against the Philistines and camped at Ebenezer, while the Philistines camped at Aphek and Israel was defeated. Israel decided to take the Ark from Shiloh for God's protection. The Ark was at Shiloh under the two sons of Eli, Hophni and Phinehas. The Philistines capture the Ark and take it from Ebenezer to Ashdod. It remains in their hands for seven months, during which time the Ark moved in three more places after Ebenezer. When the Philistine first captured the Ark at Ebenezer it caused them no end of trouble at Asdod, Gath then Ekron. Then the Ark was moved to Nob, an ancient Israelite city, during the time of Saul, the first king of Israel, where it remained for seventy-two years; while the *Tabernacle* of Moshe, the `tent of meeting', was moved from Nob to Gibeon where it remained for fifty-nine years. The Philistine engaged in several battles against the Israelite. They establish five principalities: Gaza, Asheklon, Ashdod, Ekron and Gath and they begin to call the land of Judaea Palestine, after `Philistine'.

Amongst the Philistines is a giant named `Goliath' from Gath. His height is nine feet nine inches; his weight is five hundred and forty-eight pounds; he wears a bronze helmet, a bronze armoured scale coat, bronze greaves on his legs; a bronze javelin is slung on his back; and the point of his iron spear weighs fifteen pounds. Jesse sends David, his youngest, twelve-year old son with food for his brothers. David is going back and forth tending his father's sheep. Jesse is an Ephrathite from Bethlehem in Judaea and has eight sons in all. His three older sons are part of Saul's army. David glances at the battlefield and sees Goliath threatening Saul's army. He takes out of his bag a catapult, places a stone in the sling, aims straight and precisely, the stone hits Goliath on the forehead and he falls face down. David stands over him, draws the sword of Goliath from its sheath and cuts off Goliath's head.

After years of dominance the Philistines' power begins to wane, they believe that they are cursed by the Ark and send a message to the Israelite that they wished to return the Ark to them. The men of Kiriath-jearim receive the Ark and place it into the house of Abinadab among the hills about eight miles north-east of 'Ain Shem Beth-shemesh. Eleazar son of Abinadab is consecrated to look after the Ark at Kiriath-jearim, a place also known as Balaah and Kirjath-baal. The Philistines are defeated by the Assyrians about 700 BC and they become part of the Babylonian empire. Without military power they assimilated into the surrounding cultures, reduced to commercial ventures and ceased to be a separate nation.

God raises Samuel to lead the people but he is essentially a prophet and Israel prefers to have a king instead. God directs Samuel to give them a king and Saul of the tribe of Benjamin becomes the first king of Israel. Saul is tall, handsome, humble though victorious over the Ammonites, a Semitic people closely related to the Israelite through Lot, the nephew of Abraham but more often at enmity (after Abraham and Lot had parted, Lot settled in the city of Sodom). Samuel became counsellor to Saul who selected a standing army of three thousand men. His residence was divided between Michmash and Beth-El. He put in place a garrison of one thousand men at Gibeon under the leadership of his son Jonathan. Success goes to Saul's head and he loses humility to conceit, he ceases to `reign' and resorts to `rule'; and he not only goes so far as to kill the priests at Nob but also the men, women, children and livestock. By the shedding of blood in the killing of the Gibeonites the land suffers a three-year famine, as the Gilboa mountains are also cursed by the blood that has been shed. The Israelite receive neither dew nor rain. Saul has played no part in the *Ark of Covenant,* seeped in idolatry himself as the people under his rule are oblivious to its meaning. Saul commits suicide by his own sword after his rule of forty years from 1049 BC.

Jesse is the son of Obed and his wife Unitize who is a Jewish woman and David their youngest child is anointed as king when he is eight and God promises:

> *"A shoot will come up from the stump of Jesse [David's father] and from his roots a Branch [Redeemer] will bear fruit."*

Zechariah's prophesy was that the man called the `Branch' shall bear fruit and shall build the temple of the Lord.

CHAPTER 7

THE BIBLICAL NUMBER

THE BIBLICAL NUMBER '14' has a double meaning: the numerical value of the name 'David' in ancient Jewish numerology; and to the number '7' which in ancient Jewish numerology is the number for spiritual perfection. As 14 is twice seven, it implies a double measure of virtue.

David was born to Jesse and Nitzevet bat Adel and into the illustrious family of Yishai, head of the Sanhedrin. The youngest of his family, at his birth they greeted him with derision and as a child he was separated even in the eating arrangement. He is given the task of shepherd in the hope that some wild beast would kill him but his mother understood him and knew him for what he was, *promising.* He grew to a handsome dapper little man of amiable countenance, immense physical strength and charisma. A man of war, of sensible speech, he is brave, not only did he kill Goliath when he was only a boy but also killed a lion and a bear to protect his flock. He is musical, poetical and has unshakeable faith in God. His poetic and natural love for God is reflected in deeply touching Psalms such as:

> *"The Lord is my shepherd I shall not want...my light
> and my salvation...whom should I fear...maker of heaven and
> earth..."*

When David is thirty years old Saul dies and he becomes king of Judah and Samuel becomes counsellor to David as he did for Saul. David conquers the Jebusite inhabitants and takes the city of Jebus but has had to overcome the solid defence wall around the city. He retains the beginning of the word `Je', changes `bus' to `ru', adds `salem' to `Jeru', and creates *Jerusalem* the City of David; prior to which *Salem* was a city chosen by YAHWEH from all the tribes for all the tribes of Israel, meaning *peace:* Judaism *shalom*, Islam *salaam*. David takes the Ark from the house of Abinadad and plans to take it to his city.

Amid celebrations in song, harps, tambourines, cymbals and trumpets David goes to the house of Abinadab to collect the Ark. He first wants to move the Ark to Jerusalem from Kiriath-jearim. The Kohathite priests carry the Ark on a cart driven by Uzzah and Ahio, against the normal rule that the consecrated Kohathite priests only shoulder-carry it on foot. Unfortunately, when they come to a bend on the way the oxen nearly upsets the cart and Uzza puts out his hand to steady the Ark and falls to his death. Disturbed by this incident, David decides to leave the Ark at the house of Obed-edom for three months, with the intention of moving it later to the seat of his kingdom. He pitches a tent for it in Jerusalem. Later he takes it to Jerusalem. David plans to build his *First Temple* but in a thoughtless moment he instructs his chief minister Joab and heads of the Israel community to give him a total census of the people of Israel. Joab is moved to question: *Are the people not one?* But David persists. Joab returns with the census of 1,000,000 able men of Israel and 470,000 of Judah. He did not take a census of the people of Levi and Benjamin. God is displeased at this manifestation of *splitting* the children of Israel and chastises David by the choice of three ultimatums: a three-year famine; David's enemies to overtake him in three months; or an epidemic disease to wipe out the land of Israel.

David is a man big enough to self-criticism and pleads that he alone erred and he must take the punishment, not the people but 70,000 men of Israel fall. He goes to Ornan who resides in Jerusalem and asks to buy his threshing site for six hundred shekels of gold. There David builds an Altar to God and performs prayers seeking forgiveness. God is moved and halts the destruction of Jerusalem and punishments against Israel and promises to restore Israel and vests him with the *Tabernacle* of Moshe from the ruins it had fallen into, to establish a throne in loving kindness, and a judge who would sit on it in faithfulness to seek justice and prompt righteousness.

David complains that he dwells in a house of cedar while God's *Ark of Covenant* dwells within tent curtains; that his son Solomon (a name meaning *peaceable*) is only a boy and inexperienced for the great work to be done. Solomon was born in Jerusalem about four years earlier and is David's second son by his wife Bathsheba.

Through Nathan the prophet David receives detailed plans from God. He favours a site at the top of Mount Moriah, the place where Abraham proved his readiness to offer Isaac to God. Now David builds houses for himself in Jerusalem and he pitches a tent in preparation for the *Ark of Covenant*. He proceeds to Obed-edom in Kiriath-jearim to collect the *Ark of Covenant* and places it inside the tent, they give burnt offerings and peace offerings in prayer. David continues to pursue his desire to build the *First Temple* but he is not permitted to build the temple because he has been in constant warfare and shed blood in so many wars of conquest, though defending his kingdom; and that his son Solomon is the *chosen one* to build the temple.

David assembles the Israelite at Jerusalem and they proceed to Abidadab and bring the Ark to Jerusalem where he has prepared a tent for it; not a permanent sold structure but similar to the mobile *Tabernacle* of Moshe, though in a fixed place promising it would become a full temple, for the nomadic days of the Israelite have ended. The original *Tabernacle* of Moshe is still at Gibeon, as the bronze altar which Bezalel son of Uri, the son of Hur had made. David is clothed with a robe of fine linen, an ephod of linen, with all the Levites carrying the Ark and a full entourage amid singing and with sounds of the ram's horn, trumpets, loud-sounding cymbals, harps and lyres. They give burnt offerings and peace offerings before God then David begins to lay the foundation of the *First Temple* and assembles gold, silver, bronze, iron, wood, onyx stones and other stones of various colours and kinds of precious stones and alabaster for the holy objects.

David goes further in his delight by adding the treasures of gold and silver, over and above all that he has already provided for the holy temple: 3,000 talents of gold of Ophir, and 7,000 talents of refined silver, to overlay the walls of the buildings; of gold for the things of gold and of silver for the things of silver; though the *first temple* is yet to be built. For some time now the *tabernacle* has moved from the tent-like structure that was in keeping with the nomadic existence of the Israelite but now their wandering days have long been forgotten; and David is intent on building the *First Temple*. By his love and faith in *the one true God* David *emerges* as the *specially chosen* one in the new meaning of the *tabernacle*, as it takes a significant role towards the *New Covenant* yet to be revealed.

God's purpose is manifest in the *Davidic Covenant* including the *Land Edict*. The promise is made through Nathan the prophet that a *messiah* is to come through the lineage of David and the tribe of Judah in preparation for a perpetual kingdom. No conditions are set of obedience of either David or Israel upon its fulfilment but reaffirms the promise in the previous *Abrahamic* and *Mosaic covenants*. The *messianic* significance is in the number *fourteen*, the equivalent of David's name in Hebrew. David now king of all Israel becomes first righteous king to sit on Melchizedek's throne in Jerusalem. His kingdom is most significant in the *end meaning of the tabernacle*. David prophesies that Solomon shall build the *First Temple* after which a yet to be revealed Messiah-Redeemer would be king and priest forever after the 'Order of Melchizedek': there is no genealogy for this mysterious man. Melchizedek is a role model, a typology, for *king of righteousness and peace*, and says of the yet unrevealed messiah as God's High Priest:

> "The Lord has sworn...you are a
> priest forever According
> to the order of Melchizedek."

For David's repentance God makes a statement reflecting the kingdom yet to come in a follow-up to the temporal earthly visible object in the heavenly realm:

> "When your days are complete and you lie down with
> your fathers your descendant after you ...
> he shall build a house for my name ... and I will establish
> the throne of his kingdom forever."

David is ailing and chooses his son Solomon to succeed him but there are problems for the monarchy. A conspiracy by Adonijah, Solomon's half brother, tries to deprive Solomon of the throne.

Solomon kills Adonijah and Joab, David's general, and achieves the throne two years before David dies at age seventy. David has reigned as king of Judah then of all Israel for forty years. At this time the *Ark of Covenant* is in the *Tabernacle* of David in Jerusalem, while the original *Tabernacle* of Moshe, now four hundred years old, including the original bronze wash basin is still at the high place in Gibeon.

Both tabernacles are in functional use at the same time with Zadok the priest and his family in attendance there. The prophesy of Jacob on his deathbed assigned Judah as leader and king of the Israelite has been fulfilled in King David of the tribe of Judah when all descendants of the twelve tribes submit to his reign. Solomon speaks to all the people, the commanders of thousands, the leaders and the heads of households. Then with all the assembly with him they go to the tent of meeting, the *Tabernacle of David*; there they make a thousand burnt offerings on the altar.

CHAPTER 8

SOLOMON INHERITS A POWERFUL KINGDOM

SOLOMON HAS INHERITED the throne of the most powerful kingdom of the time in an era of peace and prosperity with vast commercial enterprises and literary achievements. His kingdom extends from the Euphrates River in the north to Egypt in the south. In about 831 BC the fourth year of his reign, and at peace with his neighbours, Solomon begins the construction of the *First Temple*. Thousands of men perform the tasks required for the giant structure: cutting cedar trees from Lebanon, stones hewn at nearby quarries; ships set sail eastward and westward to bring choice materials. From Jordan bronze is cast, craftsmen brought in from neighbouring areas. YAHWEH tells Solomon to ask for whatever he wants and he asks for *wisdom to govern the people*. For that choice he is richly rewarded with wealth, wisdom, power and the ability to build a temple to the glory of YAHWEH. Solomon's extravagant construction of the *First Temple* introduced forced labour among the Israelite to quarry stone, fell trees and transport them to the site.

After seven years the *First Temple* is complete. It is not till the twelfth year of his reign that Solomon dedicates the Temple and its contents. Through efforts commenced by David, Israel has transformed the mobility of the *Tabernacle* of Moshe into the a static Temple at the Temple Mount which is also known as Mount Zion. The area of Mount Zion is first populated in the *First Temple* period but the city of David and Solomon is centred in the lower city, east and lower from Mount Zion. The Levite priests bring all the holy objects and the wooden *Ark of Covenant* from Ornan's house into the *First Temple*. Then Solomon commissions the making of another *Ark* identical to the wooden Ark of Moshe, as was in keeping with Israel's nomadic existence. The new Ark is overlaid with gold inside and out, four gold rings replace the rope ones, on the bottom of the box, on which two poles are affixed, also made of acacia wood and are coated in gold. *The Mercy Seat* above is now made of pure gold and held in place by a golden ridge or crown as a lid for closing the box from above. On the top of the *Mercy Seat* the two cherubim are beaten out of the same type of pure gold as the gold of the *Mercy Seat* and overlaid with gold inside and out.

Solomon seeks out in Gibeon the bronze altar which Bezalel the son of Uri, the son Hur had made at the tent of meeting on the threshing floor of Ornan the Jebusite; and there offers a thousand burnt animals on it. In 953 BC Solomon moves the *Tabernacle* of Moshe from Gibeon, stores it with the wooden Ark for safe keeping in the *First Temple* and there the *Tabernacle* of Moshe becomes extinct.

Solomon appoints Asaph and his relatives to be in charge of the *First Temple* and to minister continually, every day. In Obed-edom, his sixty eight relatives, the son of Jeduthun and Hosah are appointed gatekeepers. The Israelite bring daily offerings to this magnificent edifice; three times a year they gather to pay homage. Solomon immensely adds to his father's labours and his reign is a golden era when the land develops into a great centre of commerce and Jerusalem has become the centre of wisdom, riches and splendour. He collects numerous treasures and surrounds himself in luxury. He taxes his subject to the hilt, conscripts them into his army and into slave-like labour for his building projects. Solomon's wisdom spreads far and wide.

Perhaps his judgment in the incident of two women disputing over a baby is remarkable. Two women in the same house, each gave birth to a son, one baby died after a few days and the other woman exchanged the babies claiming the live baby to be hers. They argued before Solomon each claiming the baby to be hers. Solomon called for a sword and ordered that the baby be cut in two and each half to be given to each mother. One of the mothers pleaded:

> "Please do not kill my son. I love him very much, please give him to her."

The other woman said:

> "Go ahead and cut him in half, neither of us will have the baby."

Solomon gave the baby to the one who pleaded for the baby's life.
"She is his mother he said.

He is known for his writings, notably the *Song of Solomon* also known as the *Song of Songs*. A song void of law or covenant, neither does it explore wisdom like Proverbs or Ecclesiastes but celebrates sexual love, in the voices of two lovers praising each other and rejoicing in sexual intimacy. The elite and the ordinary from far and near come to gaze at the marvels of the work of Solomon; and the Israelite live in peace and harmony and are united by the *one true God.* Solomon's fame spreads far and wide and reaches Makeda, the Queen of Sheba. Unlike the typical image of Arabia, of sand dunes, camels and caravans, Sheba is far from being a barren land. Even if the shores of the Red Sea and Gulf of Aden were arid, the area mainly consisted of mountains with a cooler temperate climate. Sheba is a wealthy monarchy and Makeda is at the prime of her life and at the pinnacle of power. A visit is arranged between fellow monarchs to discuss affairs of state.

Makeda in pomp and ceremony travels to Jerusalem to behold for herself the fame of the wise King Solomon. She arrives in Jerusalem with a large retinue of escorts, servants, camels laden with spices, a great quantity of gold and precious stones as gifts for the fellow monarch. She is awed by his palace, surrounded by his courtiers and attendants behind his livery, scrumptious varieties of food on the table, his cup bearers in a variety of flowing wines and his lavish offerings in the *First Temple,* an opulent copy of Moshe's original *Tabernacle.*

Makeda is moved to say that what she has seen herself surpasses what she had heard about his wisdom and achievements. Her gracious host Solomon gives her a first hand tour of the *First Temple*, his exquisite gardens of rare flowers ornamented with pools and fountains and the splendours of the architecture of government buildings and palace. A lavish banquet is prepared in her honour but the cook was too generous in `spicing' the goat stew. At the end of the banquet Makeda retires to her guest wing attended by her handmaids and extra provided by her host. She is tossing and turning, the heat of the spices is breathing back at her and she cannot sleep. She wanders out of her rooms into some ante chamber looking for water to cool her burning throat and she finds water in an earthen pot. As she is drinking the water Solomon finds her, gently grabs her wrist and says:

"*You are taking something that belongs to me...*"

The visit is over and as Makeda entered Jerusalem in pomp and ceremony, so is her departure for Sheba. There she finds that she is blessed with the *Maternal Covenant* and gives birth to a son. He is named Ibn-al-Malik, known as Menelik. Makeda is so inspired by Solomon that she spreads his faith in Sheba and neighbouring areas and Judaism becomes the faith of her realm. When Menelik turns twenty-two years old he learns his true identity from his mother, that his father is King Solomon and she permits his wish to visit his father in Jerusalem. Solomon receives his son most graciously and Menelik stays with his father for three years during which time he learns the Law of Moshe. The people become jealous of Menelik and they ask Solomon to send him home. Solomon agrees but with the conditions that each of the eldest sons of the high priests, plus one thousand people from each tribe of Judah, accompany Menelik home. They agree. It is done. Menelik requests and Solomon commissions a replica of the *Ark of Covenant* for Menelik to take back with him to Ethiopia. It is now 950 BC Makeda dies and Menelik succeeds her with a new title of *Emperor and King of Kings of Ethiopia*. Like his mother he practises and spreads Judaism. He founds the Solomonic Dynasty of Ethiopia and he becomes known as *Son of the Wise*.

****

SOLOMON HAS BEEN GIFTED with wisdom and done many wonderful great things and as lavish in all things: seven hundred wives and three hundred concubines, among whom are also non-

Judaeans unlike his father David who had seven spouses. Solomon marries Tachere, a daughter of Pharaoh, for political alliance with Egypt which increases trade. The daughters of Pharaohs did not marry outside their own family, nor did the Israelite out of the Jewish community. But Solomon is unique. He does not do things in `half measures', he is one of the greatest contributors to the population of Israel if not the only greatest one at the time. Intimacy is reflected in the *Song of Songs* particularly inspired by Tachere. Together they recite:

Solomon:
> "I have compared thee, O my love, to a steed before
> Pharaoh's chariots."

Tachere:
> "I am dark ...because the sun has tanned me ...my mother's
> sons ...made me keeper of the vineyards..."

Out of his vast harem Tachere is the wife singled out and her influence over him is the beginning of his downfall. Solomon is increasingly influenced into the worship of idols, the Egyptian way. The *Ark of Covenant* on which he lavished so much gold loses its meaning to him and his people, despite his father's counsel on the importance of the worship of the *one true God.* At the end of Solomon's reign Israel becomes spiritually lacking followed by deterioration and the *First Temple* is neglected. He has ruled until 931 BC and dies in 924 BC.

AFTER SOLOMON'S DEATH the kingdom was divided. Ten tribes formed the kingdom of Israel (930-722 BC), in a succession of twenty kings. Judah and Benjamin formed the kingdom of Judah (933-586 BC), also followed by a succession of twenty kings. Most of the kings practised idolatry, the worst served Baal. The importance of the *Ark of Covenant* and the *First Temple* featured in varying degrees: slightly or not at all despite some repairs to it being carried out by a few of the kings. Some features included king Jehoash's (of Judah) building a pagan altar on the pattern of an Assyrian pagan altar in Damascus and placing it near the *First Temple.* making burnt sacrifice offering at the new altar, reserving the bronze altar for himself where he carried out sacrifices to the gods of Damascus. He took treasures from the *First Temple* and sent them to Uriah as a model to build altars for himself on every corner of Jerusalem; he removed the bronze altars and the holy objects from the *First Temple* to comply with the demands of the king of Assyria as a present to him in Damascus. King Ahab marries the infamous Jezebel which deepens his idolatry; and he builds a temple to the Canaanite deity Baal popularising idolatry among the Jewish people.

Hezekiah was one of the better kings of Judah as in the first year of his reign he restored the *First Temple* of Solomon to full worship. Josiah became king of Judah when he was eight years old after the assassination of his father and ruled for thirty-one years (641-610 BC) . He was steadfast in his faith in YAHWEH and walked in the footsteps of his ancestor king David. During his eighteenth year of reign he took steps to repair the *First Temple*.

Rehoboam, his son by Naamah of the Ammonites, is forty-one years old and becomes king and rules in Jerusalem. In about 920 BC in the fifth year of Rehoboam's reign Shishak, king of Egypt, comes to Jerusalem and loots the treasures of the *First Temple* including all the shields of gold which Solomon had made. Rehoboam and the people under his reign pay homage to Asherah the mother goddess who is called 'the creator of the gods'. Along with her are Astarte and Anath, three great goddesses of the Canaanite who descend from Ham, second son of Noah, father of thirty nations. They build high places and sacred pillars on every high hill in honour of Asherah.

They indulge in wanton practices, Rehoboam is oblivious to the existence of the *Ark of Covenant*, its whereabouts or its meaning; and he does not follow what his forefathers practised. YAHWEH is much displeased by Rehoboam's and the activities of the people under his rule. In about 931 BC Jeroboam was chosen spokesman for most of the tribes of Israel and leading a group of people confronts Rehoboam with a demand for lighter taxes. When he refuses their demand, ten tribes of the Israelite reject Rehoboam and David's dynasty and the kingdom was divided – oblivous to the *Ark of Covenant.*

CHAPTER 9

AFTER SOLOMON'S DEATH

THE ISAELITE HAD GONE through a nomadic existence to a more settled life for hundreds of years, they settled in Palestine, won and lost an empire; and they had seen the glory of Solomon's magnificent *Temple* which had endured for three hundred seventy-three years. But the reign of king of Israel Hoshea (732-722 BC) saw the beginning of Assyrian conquest of Israel, leading to a forced *en masse* exile of the Israelite later and forever more to be known as the *lost tribes*. Towards the end of the rule of the last king Zedekia of Judah (597-586 BC) followed the total destruction of the *First Temple* by king of the Babylonians at the fall of Jerusalem.

Nabopolassar provided for his son Nebuchadnezzar II a stable base and ample wealth on which to build on to the son's fullest advantage He was king of the Babylonian and an idol worshipper. He invaded, destroyed the *First Temple* of Solomon and looted all the treasures within. He burned the *Temple,* the palace and all the houses of Jerusalem, after the Siege of Jerusalem of 587 BC. When Babylon was captured by Alexander III (The Great) he only had the time to take a few choice captives, such as Daniel, the Biblical prophet in 605 BC.

Darius confirmed his interest by returning the sacred objects which had been taken from the *First Temple* and built a *Second Temple*, replacing Solomon's Temple, which stood for 420 years (349 BCE-70 CE). In 165 BC Matthias 1 of the Maccabees, restored the *Second Temple* to full worship. During some periods of interests in the semi restorations of the temple the meaning of *Tabernacle* and *Ark of Covenant* was unknown to them and appeared to be dormant but *not extinct* intrinsically.

It was not till after a three-month siege that the city was taken by

Julius Caesar in 45 BC after he defeated Pompey in Alexandria, in his attempt to resolve the Egyptian Civil War between Ptolemy XIII and his sister Cleopatra. The Romans brought the region of Judaea under them; and in an attempt to minimise Jewish attachment to the land they use the term *Palestinia* to refer to the region.

****

IN THE CONTINUATION OF THE HUMAN DRAMA Herod was cast as a despotic powerful tyrant in Judaea. Known as Herod the Great, ethnically Arab and a converted Jew, though not of the Davidic line, he was not accepted by the Jewish people. He was made `King of the Jews' by the Roman Senate (about 7 BC). Jealous and angry at the news that a `king to be' is born, he commanded that all children from age two and under, in and around Bethlehem be killed. Yosef and Miriam took Yeshua and fled to Egypt where they remained. Herod carried out his threat and many innocents were killed.

The fugitives heard that stricken by a deadly disease Herod was dead and they returned to Nazareth, Judaea. The baby was saved. Upon Herod's death the Romans divided his kingdom among three of his sons and his sister as tetrarchs (each of four rulers). Herod Antipas became tetrarch of Galilee (4BC-39AD).

****

ROME APPOINTED HIGH PRIESTS to serve the *Second Temple* at Jerusalem and cunningly rearranged religious interests of Jews and the political interests of Rome in a coalition; imposed taxation, property census for tax purposes and taxes on ancestral land held and exalted in Jewish ideology. In 6 CE Jews opposed the rise of Roman laws in the fear of appropriation by Rome which led to the crucifixion of over 2,000 insurgents and selling into slavery of 20,000 Jews. Intense opposition to Rome came from Galilee, the centre of an armed resistance movement of Zealots. Continued Jewish opposition led Rome to regard Jewish nationalism and religious fervour as a threat to law and order. They appoint local leaders to govern and the Roman Senate designates Herod as King of the Jews. He became the ruler of Galilee under Rome, constructed the city of Tiberius on the western shore of Galilee in 19 CE, and forced the peasant population to meet heavier tax burdens to pay for it. As Herod I the Great he was the most notorious of the rulers who transformed the country; refurbished Bebron, Jericho, adorned many cities and erected many heathen temples. He built the port of Caesarea on the coast and a temple to Augustus in Samaria.

In the eighteenth year of his reign about 20 BC Herod decided to rebuild a Temple on the ruins of Solomon's *First Temple* at Jerusalem, on a rather magnificent scale.

The sons of Herod King of the Jews also became regional rulers: Herod Antipas ruled Galilee in the north and Herod, Philip I, ruled in the south. Then the Romans decide to appoint their own governors to Judaea but local agents collect the taxes, to which the latter made a profit by adding their own fees to the resentment of the people. It was a time manifesting a confusion of cultures, the effect of a succession of ruling powers, each bringing influences of its own culture in a multifaceted cosmopolitan and a secular existence.

****

GALILEAN SOCIETY in the Judaea of the first century AD is comprised of the higher socio-economic strata: the Roman imperial aristocracy; the ruling class of Palestine; the Herodian client kings; and the ordinary people. Hebrew as a common language somewhat altered due to foreign influence; Greek, Aramaic and Syrian become the dominant languages. The Israelite fit the category of nomads who entered Canaan with Joshua; their culture is Jewish and their language is Hebrew. By this time many Israelite had become scattered among the nations of the world to blend with the genes of those countries; some never forgot or gave up their faith.

Jerusalem-born historian Josephus Flavius and Roman scholar Pliny the Elder tell us that the Qumran community lived an ascetic life and were waiting for God's apocalyptic intervention in human history. It may be unlikely that Yeshua had any contact with this particular group. Still, he was introduced to the ascetical option through his contact with the disciples of John the Baptist who represented a quasi-Essenic withdrawal from mainstream society.

The followers of John the Baptist included the competing systems of Sadducee, Pharisees,were in many ways idealists of Jewish society who made up of most of the Scribes, the theologians of the day; Essenes, Zealots and followers of other charismatic leaders. Each group had a particular way of interpreting the Hebrew scriptures and applying them to the present. What kept these diverse philosophical and religious groups together was their common Jewish practices, such as following dietary restrictions (*kashrut*), holding weekly Sabbaths and worshipping at the *Second Temple* in Jerusalem, the birthplace of Judaism and Christianity.

They are a people with a common problem as most oppressed peoples in a deep spiritual conviction. This is because they kept the flame of oral testimonies of their patriarchs, Abraham, Isaac, Jacob and later Moshe, victims than victors in their fight for national sovereignty. Yeshua was a Palestinian Jew much imbued with the stories of foreign invasions that sought to subjugate the Jewish people, and the successful self-rule under the Hebrew kings. Of historical interest is the fact that the Temple was destroyed by the Romans in 70 CE.

However, Yeshua was more than a teacher. He was also prophet, miracle-worker, healer, defender of the poor and oppressed. Jesus' distinctiveness needs to be appreciated in the context of his Jewish life and times. This was a context in which religion and politics were intertwined in a much more complex way than we think of them today, a consequence of a succession of empires by different rulers practising their own distinct customs and culture imposed upon subjugated peoples of any area. Where prayers are performed is the Temple of Herod not regarded as the `First Temple', the `Second' or the `Third' but rather the *Temple,* this too, has evolved as the people and their culture.

The contemporary society is not in any way touched by the

Tabernacle of Moshe or the whereabouts of the *Ark of Covenant*, seemingly all phased out into history but *intrinsically* not so. It is now in the reign of Tiberius Caesar, Pontius Pilate who served under Tiberius as prefect, is the fifth Prefect of the Roman province of Judaea, and jointly rules Galilee with Herod Antipas. The administration of Judaea is a two-tier system shared between Rome and the Jewish leaders who exercise control in the name of Rome and share a strong alliance, the system by which the Herod family grew to prominence. Later Pontius Pilate becomes governor of Judaea.

Caiphas was one of the most influential men in Jerusalem an outstanding political operator and a Jewish high priest of the *Second Temple.* His power base is the Sanhedrin, the supreme council of Jews which controls civil and religious law over which he presides. He is in good standing with Pontius Pilate. Roman leaders pay close attention to the *Second Temple* activity which in Jerusalem serves several purposes, as both the revered centre of religious life, a place for prayers and sacrifices, and as a central bank, a place for taxes and tithes.

The Pharisees control the synagogues, they are the democratic, progressive new party of the ordinary people and mostly influential in the area of religious devotion and daily ritual, more like a family than a religious sect. They are in the majority about 5,000 in Palestine and represent the rulers and the official order mostly resident in Jerusalem. The Sadducees represent the privileged, conservative, traditional elite of Judaism and also combine the legislature, executive and judicial powers constituting the national parliament. The scribal Pharisee are represented on the Sanhedrin but the power rests with the Sadducee. The Sanhedrin is an all civil, criminal, political, social and religious body as a high court of justice supreme tribunal of the Jews comprising seventy members.

There is much hostility between the two groups. The Pharisees oppose Roman rule and openly challenge the privileged status of the Sadducee and criticise their easy tolerance of foreign rule. In Judaea the connecting medium of money is not unlike the confusion of languages and cultures. The coins are Roman, Greek,

Syrian and Jewish. The Jews are allowed to issue coins only in bronze, Roman assarion (one cent). Large sums are expressed in talents and minas. The Syrian stater, about 50 cents; Roman denarius, 20 cents, the Greek drachma, is equivalent to denarius; and the stater is accepted as equal to the Jewish shekel 1/50 of a mina; and about 65 cents for two persons as tax to use the *Temple*. The denarius is the usual day's wage for a labourer in the field and it is also the coin of tax to the Emperor. Quadrants: 1/4 of a cent is the Jewish perutah or lepton, which is worth 1/8 of a cent – the famous *widow's mite*.

****

JULIUS CAESAR (100-44 BC), the great soldier, conqueror, classical writer of Roman prose, lawyer, politician, statesman and dictator of the Roman Republic, started it all in the currency system. He took back from the money changers the power to coin money and then minted coins for the benefit of `all'.

With this new vision, there was a large supply of money. He established many massive construction projects and public works and won the love of the common people. But the money changers hated him for it; and his colleagues, including his beloved Brutus, ended his life by sticking daggers into his body.

After his death plentiful money ended in Rome, taxes increased, as did corruption. Roman money supply became reduced by 90 percent, the consequences were the common people lost lands and money.

When the Jews come to the *Temple* at Jerusalem they can only pay their entrance with a special coin, the `half shekel', the equivalent of half an ounce of silver. It is the only coin at this time of pure silver and of assured weight without the image of a pagan Emperor but according to the Jews it is the only coin acceptable to YAHWEH.

CHAPTER 10

Yochanan is born to Elikana & Elesheba

LIKE MOST JEWISH CHILDREN Yochanan had been nurtured and imbued with a sense of destiny by his parents, Zachariah and Eleshaba. Yochanan is now about thirty years old, he is on the banks of the Jordan River, and begins to preach against the current evils. He attracts large crowds and one of his followers is Shim'on (Simon, meaning `he has heard').

Likewise, Yeshua has been brought up by his parents Yosef and Miriam in the Jewish tradition. Education was a priority for Jewish people. He lived most of his life in the small village of Nazareth within the province of Galilee, very much a Jewish enclave close to the metropolitan centres of Tiberius and Sepphoris. It was also relatively poor and overpopulated; there was a scarcity

of natural resources such as water and fertile soil though Nazareth could not be called destitute. Jesus came from a family of craftsmen or carpenters which suggests a reasonable socio-economic standard of living. Yeshua was well versed in the Scriptures and the Jewish tradition, like most children of his time he was attached to a local teacher learning the Torah in Hebrew. When he is about twelve years old he goes to the synagogue in Jerusalem on the Feast of Passover on Shabbath; and the leaders are awed by his extraordinary knowledge and understanding of the Scriptures.

Ancient scrolls reveal that Yeshua spent seventeen years in India and Tibet, from the age thirteen, where he was both a student and teacher of Buddhist and Hindu holy men at Jaganath, Puri, India. The story of his journey from Jerusalem to Benares was recorded by Brahman historians. Up to the present they still know Yeshua and love him as St Issa. At age approximately twenty-nine Yeshua returned to Nazareth, where he lived with his parents and worked as a carpenter in the shop of his father Yosef.

****

THE FIRST IMPORTANT MOVEMENT to arise in Galilee was led by Yochanan, apocalyptic visionary and revolutionist. He focuses upon the importance of *baptism* and calls upon his followers to repent and confess their sins, live and follow a good lifestyle, and prepare for the imminent coming of an avenging God. He becomes well-known and popular.

The Pharisees and the Sadducee come to Yochanan to be baptised and he refers to them as a *generation of vipers.* He baptises them, nonetheless, and tells them that there is one yet to come who shall baptise with the Holy Spirit and fire to empower those who already have had the water baptism of repentance of sin.

A young man of about twenty-nine years old travels from Galilee to the River Jordan to be baptised by Yochanan who had never met the young man before and it is the *most remarkable moment* of Yochanan's ministry. Yochanan recognised Yeshua as sinless and says:

"*It is I who needs to be baptised by you*".

After a discourse on who has the greater authority to baptise, Yochanan agrees to baptise Yeshua, a baptism that takes place in *adulthood.* Yeshua departs to preach in Galilee and Yochanan continues preaching in the Jordan

Valley. Yeshua is led up by the spirit into the wilderness to be tempted by Satan and there he fasts for forty days and forty nights and he becomes hungry. Satan appears to him and tempts him to demonstrate his supernatural powers as proof of his divinity and indicates three temptations: turn the stones into bread and eat; jump off a cliff and let the angels catch him; and surrender to Satan by receiving his kingdom as a reward. Yeshua resisted the devil and put him in his place. Yeshua by his resistance demonstrated the vital spiritual principle of "Submit therefore to God. Resist the devil and he will flee from you." And, the angels bring him nourishment.

****

HEROD HAS A LIAISON WITH HERODIAS, the wife of his brother, Herod Philip I, able ruler over the former north eastern quarter of their father's kingdom of Judaea. Herod divorces his wife Phasaelis and Herodias divorces her husband so Herod and Herodias can marry.

Yochanan publicly disapproves of this because they both discarded their spouses and marrying an ex-husband's brother is regarded as adultery. In Hebrew law, the wife is to marry the husband's brother provided the husband has died. This in fact is a requirement to marry the next kinsman to carry on the line of the husband.

Combined by his anger and Herod's phobia of the rising popularity of Yochanan he orders an arrest and imprisonment of Yochanan; but he does not put him to death because he fears repercussions from the masses who regard Yochanan as a prophet. Soon after, Herod celebrates his birthday, and puts on a lavish banquet for his high-ranking officials, military officers and the elite of Galilee. Salome, beautiful damsel, the daughter of Herodias, lives in the palace. The elaboration of the Biblical version is that she danced the dance of the seven veils before the king and his guests. In provocative sways and twirls of her youthful graceful figure. Herod, as his guests, is inflamed, he is in a state of drunkenness filled with longing and desire, he cries:

> "Ask me whatever you want...including half of my kingdom
>
> and they are yours..."

The damsel, influenced by her mother Herodias who hates Yochanan for criticising her liaison with her brother-in-law, asks for the head of Yochanan on a platter. Herod is appalled but his desire for the damsel overcomes all reasoning and he promises her wish. Yochanan is beheaded in the prison cell. His head is brought on a platter and is given to the damsel and she carries it to her mother. The disciples of Yochanan come and take his body for burial and post haste they go to Yeshua and tell him what has happened. When he hears this Yeshua withdraws to a solitary place for a while. During the time John was in prison, Yeshua had already started His ministry.

****

YESHUA IS WALKING ALONG LAKE GALILEE and sees two fishermen brothers, Shim'on (Hebrew origin, Simon) and Andreas (Greek name) casting a net into the lake and Yeshua invites them to follow him and be *fishers of men*. They drop their nets and follow him. Yeshua renames Shim'on `Petros', meaning `rock' in the Greek language. Then another called John, also a fisherman, follows. Others follow and eventually form a group of four led squads. Simon Peter: Andrew, James of Zebedee and John; Philip: Bartholomew, Thomas and Matthew, the tax collector; James of Alphaeus: Thaddeus, Simon the Canaanite, and Judas Iscariot. Yeshua is not selective as to any particular theological, gender or other qualifications but gathers around just plain ordinary men and women from different walks of life.

In the first century world Yeshua's treatment of women is rather revolutionary, as he makes no distinctions as to who is to follow him or in healing those in need of healing.

Women are making a great contribution to his ministry and they include Mary Magdalene; Joanna; Susanna; Mary mother of James; Salome (not Herodian's daughter), mother of Zebedee and sister of Miriam, mother of Yeshua; Mary the wife of Clopas; and others. They follow him.

Yeshua sits down and the disciples come and surround him as he begins to teach them, listened to by the multitude. He delivers the *Sermon on the Mount* under the *New Covenant*; a central expression of his teachings in a New Age of Dispensation. He has come to proclaim; and interprets the *Old Covenant* or *Mosaic Covenant*; he confirms, expands and analyses the *Ten Commandments*, it is the most famous sermon ever given by anyone in all time. The *Sermon on the Mount* in a nutshell:

"Do unto others as you would wish them to do unto you.
"Judge not lest ye be judged."

Then Yeshua tells his disciples of the *Five Trees of Paradise* and says one who has existed from the beginning before he comes to be is blessed. If they are his students and listen to his words, the stones around them would become their servants and would minister to them: for there are `Five Trees' in Paradise, which do not move in summer or in winter, and their leaves do not fall down and are ever green: `unchangeable'. Whoever knows them will not taste death. The *Five Trees of Paradise* are: life, immortality, comprehension, knowledge, and knowledge of good and evil. They refer to the benefits of `self-awareness', knowledge of one's true nature by which we are able to understand Yeshua's symbolic language and master external reality.

In addition, are the physical five-sense organs within the image of God which the body carries; and our knowledge of the external world depends on the kinds and quality of our perception through the five senses and the key is `discernment', they are:

Sight, the eye is the organ of vision; you see the speck that is in your brother's eye, but you do not see the beam that is in your own eye. When you take the beam out of your own eye, then you will see clearly to take the speck out of your brother's eye. Love your brother like your soul and protect that person like the pupil of your eye – not necessarily a biological sibling but any `fellow human being.

Here the meaning is not literal as the `eye sees' but perception in making capital of the faults of another while ignoring our own:

"If you do not judge you will not be judged."

Smell, the nose is the organ that has the sense of smell.

Taste, the receptors for taste, called taste buds, are situated chiefly in the tongue, but they are also located in the roof of the mouth and near the pharynx.

Touch, the sense of touch is distributed throughout the body.

Sound, the ear is the organ of hearing, not confined to `sound' but what we perceive from what we hear. [Collectively the above are the essence of mind and each is distributed throughout the body.]

****

THREE DAYS BEFORE THE PASSOVER **Y**eshua and his followers travel to Jerusalem to celebrate the *Feast of Passover.* They find the sacred city overflowing with thousands of pilgrims from different parts of the world. The Temple fee charge brings in large revenues. The reason for celebration of the Passover is important as a time when God brought the Israelite out of Egyptian bondage into the Holy land as an end to foreign oppression. Despite the changes that have taken place, the significance of the Passover remains unchanged for the Jew in their rituals in the worship of YAHWEH. Visitors entering Jerusalem have first to undergo the *Mikveh* (Hebrew), the new ritual of immersion in the waters of the Jordan River for purification and forgiveness of sin, as presented by John the Baptist to the Temple of Herod. In the evening before the feast of the Passover Yeshua had sent one of the disciples to book a room with an inn-keeper where they could have supper. While they were eating he said:

> *"I have earnestly desired to eat this Passover with you before I suffer".*

He symbolises his body to unleavened bread which he breaks, gives thanks, and gives it to his disciples:

> *"This is my body which is given to you in remembrance of me."*

Yeshua is like the unleavened bread, unpuffed, without pride; not with old leaven, or with the leaven of malice and wickedness, but with the unleavened bread of sincerity and truth.

Then Yeshua symbolises wine as his blood in a cup, gives thanks and says:

> *"This is the token of God's new covenant to save you – an agreement sealed with the blood I have poured out for you."*

Yeshua rises from supper, posing as a servant, pours water into a basin and begins to wash the disciples' feet. He starts with the *feet of Judas.* After this they go out.

****

YESHUA IS SCOURGED by the Roman soldiers and made to carry his cross to the place of execution, he is fatigued from beating to carry his cross (or beam?) all the way, as he is taunted and humiliated by the crowds. The Roman soldiers impel a black man, Simon of Cyrene, to carry the cross through the `Dolorosa' (Latin for `way of sorrow' or `way of pain') out of Jerusalem to Golgotha – Aramaic meaning `the skull', or `Calvary' in the Latin language. Jewish law does not permit crucifixions and burials to take place inside the city. Simon is of African descent and Cyrene is a Roman district of Cyrenaica, in the northern coast of the African continent settled by the Greeks in 630 BC, later infused with other populations: Jewish, Romans and Greek-speaking Hellenistic Jews.

In addition to the centurion and other soldiers guarding those being crucified, standing are Miriam, Yeshua's mother; Mary Magdalene; Mary the mother of James and Joseph; the mother of Zebedee's sons; Mary the wife of Clopas; and Salome. Also, watching from a distance, are many women who have been following Yeshua during his ministry, and he is crucified along with two thieves, one on either side. Crucifixion is reserved for criminals and slaves and is the worst `barbaric' mode of execution imposed upon the guilty by the (so-called) civilised Romans. Yeshua, as the two thieves, is nailed to a cross (or tied with rope on a stake?) and hangs there until his own weight suffocates him.

Yeshua sees his mother and the disciple John and says to his mother:

   "Woman, behold your son."

To John he says:

   "Man, behold your mother"

One does not have to be biologically related to regard another as a parent, sibling or child. Whatever Yeshua does is not about himself but for others.

****

FROM THE SIXTH to the ninth hour - three o'clock in the afternoon - there was darkness all over the land. God had turned away because the Almighty could not look upon sin. Around the ninth hour, Yeshual cried in a loud voice:

"Father into Thy hands I commit my spirit."

He gave up the spirit and breathed his last. The death of Yeshua is symbolic to the death of every human. At the moment Yeshua died the earth quaked and the rocks split. The *Land Edict,* part of the *Davidic Covenant* which pertained to the earthly land became extinct; the *Veil* (symbolised to the body of Yeshua) that separated the *Holy Place* and the Holy *of the Holies rent* and the *way opened* for child o the promise to the place of the *skilled artist:* the *Promised Land.*

Epilogue

By the regeneration of God's beautiful ornament through genes our ancestors live on in us, as we shall live on in posterity, even the childless for they share genes with siblings and cousins, Though there is the tendency for man to stay rooted in the ego of the present and not look beyond – is regeneration not 'resurrection'?

www.ingramcontent.com/pod-product-compliance
Lightning Source LLC
Chambersburg PA
CBHW070134100426
42744CB00009B/1835